W9-CCR-291

Traditional Kitchen Wisdom

"To forget how to dig the earth and tend the soil
is to forget ourselves."

—MAHATMA GANDHI

• BACK TO BASICS •

Traditional Kitchen Wisdom

Techniques and Recipes for Living a Simpler, More Sustainable Life

EDITED BY ANDREA CHESMAN

The Reader's Digest Association, Inc.
Pleasantville, New York | Montreal

A READER'S DIGEST BOOK

Copyright © 2010 Quintet Publishing Limited

This book was designed and produced by Quintet Publishing Limited,
6 Blundell Street, London N7 9BH, UK

FOR QUINTET PUBLISHING
Project Editor Asha Savjani
Illustrator Bernard Chau
Art Editor Zoe White
Additional Text Carly Beckerman, Sula Paolucci
Designer Anna Plucinska
Art Director Michael Charles
Managing Editor Donna Gregory
Publisher James Tavendale

FOR READER'S DIGEST
U.S. Project Editor Kim Casey
Manager, English Book Editorial, Reader's Digest Canada Pamela Johnson
Canadian Consulting Editors Jesse Corbeil, J. D. Gravenor
Copy Editor Barbara McIntosh Webb
Project Designer Jennifer Tokarski
Senior Art Director George McKeon
Executive Editor, Trade Publishing Dolores York
Associate Publisher, Trade Publishing Rosanne McManus
President and Publisher, Trade Publishing Harold Clarke

Library of Congress Cataloging-in-Publication Data
Back to basics / edited by Andrea Chesman.
    p. cm.
  Includes index.
  ISBN 978-1-60652-056-7
1. Home economics--United States--Handbooks, manuals, etc.   2. Sustainable living-
-Handbooks, manuals, etc. I. Chesman, Andrea. II. Reader's digest.
  TX23. B32 2009
  640--dc22
                                        2009028254

All images are the copyright of Quintet Publishing Ltd. While every effort has
been made to credit contributors, Quintet Publishing would like to apologize
if there have been any omissions or errors—and would be pleased to make the
appropriate corrections for future editions of the book.

Note to Our Readers
The editors who produced this book have attempted to make the contents as
accurate and correct as possible. Illustrations, photographs, and text have been
carefully checked. All instructions should be reviewed and understood by the reader
before undertaking any project.

All do-it-yourself activities involve a degree of risk. Although the editors have made
every effort to ensure accuracy, the reader remains responsible for the selection and
use of materials and methods. Always follow manufacturer's instructions and observe
safety precautions.

We are committed to both the quality of our products and the service we provide to
our customers. We value your comments, so please feel free to contact us.

The Reader's Digest Association, Inc.
Adult Trade Publishing
Reader's Digest Road
Pleasantville, NY 10570-7000

For more Reader's Digest products and information,
visit our website:
www.rd.com (in the United States)
www.readersdigest.ca (in Canada)

QTT.BCK

Printed in China

10 9 8 7 6 5 4 3 2 1

CONTENTS

INTRODUCTION

There was a time not so long ago when most households tended a kitchen garden, kept a flock of chickens pecking in the backyard, and milked a family cow. On hot summer days, the women of the family gathered to "put up" jams and pickles, and thirst-quenching homemade beverages were brought out to the fields where the menfolk toiled. Dinners were made from scratch, and families sat down together to break bread. This lifestyle was not only sustainable, it was also joyous, connecting the people who lived this way to their past, to their future, and to the land that nurtured them.

BACK TO BASICS

Call it going back to basics, a greening of the home, a return to the traditional, or doing it yourself. Today, having a sustainable home has become very important once again. For some people, growing and preserving food is an economic necessity; others are motivated by a concern for the environment; still others are eager for the simple pleasures of gardening and to restore the hearth as the center of the household. The motivation may also be prompted by a desire to eat with the seasons, enjoying food that is free from artificial flavors and chemicals—food that tastes as if it came from the good earth and not from some vat of chemicals.

Whether you are looking to save money spent on groceries, assure the quality of the food you provide for your family, or eat locally year-round, it makes sense to grow and preserve your own food. Not so long ago, our forebears learned these valuable skills of self-sufficiency; now, perhaps, it's time to listen to what our grandparents can teach us about skills for self-reliance that will serve us in good times and bad. There is something immensely satisfying about being personally involved in every step of the process—from seed to plate.

Fortunately for us, modern appliances, including dishwashers, food processors, and food dehydrators, whittle away hours from the process of stocking the pantry, while freezer jams and pickles make preserving easy and

fast. On the other hand, there is a tendency to start new projects by buying tools and appliances that are quickly abandoned. Remember that you do not have to invest a lot of money or buy every new tool or gadget to make your house more self-reliant. You don't even need to own land. The burgeoning of farmers' markets means that everyone can have ready access to fresh and organic produce, whether you live in big cities or small towns.

YOU DON'T HAVE TO DO EVERYTHING YOURSELF

Everything from gardening to preserving can be done more efficiently if you enlist your friends to share in the labor and the rewards. Children can be assigned simple tasks, such as weeding or shelling peas. In addition to supplying extra hands, they are sponges for learning new skills and will later thank you for teaching them about self-reliance, something children have been missing in recent years.

In the end, the goal is to live on less and still have plenty—plenty of food, plenty of fun, plenty of skills, plenty of self-confidence to face an uncertain world. This book will help you get started on that very rewarding path.

PLANNING AND PLANTING YOUR KITCHEN GARDEN

Y ou don't have to have a green thumb to plant a garden. You don't need acres of land to make your household more self-sufficient. All you need is a sunny corner on a balcony or a small patch of soil in the front or backyard and a desire to participate in the growing and harvesting of the food you enjoy. Make your meals healthier and more delicious by growing fruit and vegetables, or choose to plant flowers for fragrant and beautiful decoration.

Planning your kitchen garden is simple. There are a few key guidelines to consider, and learning the basics will help you decide what you really want out of your plots or in your pots. Planting is the next step, and there are different methods and techniques, depending on what you would like to grow. Do you need a raised bed? What type of soil should you use? Find out all the answers to your questions, and start planning and planting your kitchen garden today.

THE KITCHEN GARDEN

A kitchen garden can be a small plot of land devoted to growing all the vegetables, fruits, and herbs you need, but it can also be much, much smaller—perhaps a collection of pots and window boxes set strategically on a balcony or deck. Or you may just want to continue to devote your gardening efforts to the flowers you love and intersperse a few food plants—say, tomatoes and peppers—among the perennials, with perhaps a row of salad greens forming a decorative, edible border.

PLANNING

Begin planning a garden by considering what food plants you might want to grow. Do you live on salads all through the summer? Do you cook with lots of herbs? Are you hoping to stock your freezer for the winter ahead? Are you interested in growing foods that keep for long periods of time with a minimum amount of processing, like winter squash?

Do you want to grow fruit? Small fruit like strawberries, blueberries, and raspberries can easily fit into a kitchen garden.

Do you want fresh flowers, too? Yes, flowers can be included in a kitchen garden, and some, like nasturtiums and chive blossoms, make excellent additions to a salad. So get started by making a list of everything you hope to grow.

Do you want fresh herbs? A small plot can accommodate fragrant staples, such as thyme, parsley, basil, and sage. Or grow your own mint for a fresh touch for your lemonade or tea.

HOW DOES MY GARDEN GROW?

With tomatoes! That's the most popular vegetable among home gardeners. Right behind tomatoes are lettuces and leafy greens, green beans, and summer squash and zucchini. These vegetables are particularly easy to grow. But don't forget broccoli, cucumbers, carrots, radishes, and herbs.

You may wish to avoid vegetables that are space hogs (pumpkins and winter squash) or are available as staples year-round (potatoes and onions). But, if these crops are important to you, or if you want to try varieties that are not available in the supermarket, go ahead and grow them. They aren't particularly fussy vegetables to grow.

Drawing Plans

The next step is finding a site for your garden. Vegetables require full sun for at least six hours a day, but more if possible. The site needs to be as flat as possible, but you can build a terraced garden if you must use a hillside. Ideally the garden needs to be convenient to both water and the house. Deep, well-drained soil is best for vegetables, but chances are you will have to build up the soil, so don't let poor soil stop you.

In drier climates, you will need to consider how to water your garden. Soaker hoses work well, but you must be able to attach the hose to a nearby spigot.

A kitchen garden can be as small as a couple of containers of herbs or salad greens and potted tomato plants, or as large as an acre or more. For a small family, a garden in the range of 20 square feet (2 sq m) is a manageable size for one person to handle, and will yield a surprisingly large and varied harvest.

Once you have selected your site and decided on a size, use a pencil to draw an outline of the area on a piece of graph paper.

SPACE-SAVING TIPS

If your soil is fertile, consider planting crops in succession. You can harvest fast-maturing peas, spinach, and radishes and then plant green beans, chard, beets, kale, or brussels sprouts in the same spot. Sow lettuce and other greens every two weeks for harvesting throughout the season. In areas with mild winters, you may be able to plant three crops by following your fall crop with a hardy vegetable, such as collards.

Remember, your kitchen garden is a part of your landscape, so plan it to please the eye, putting the flowers where they can be seen and keeping the rows and paths neat and orderly. If your space is very limited, consider growing vertically by adding trellises, fences, or teepees to support space-hogging vines, such as cucumbers and pole beans. Even a bag of planting mix can become an instant planter by cutting square openings in one of the long, flat sides.

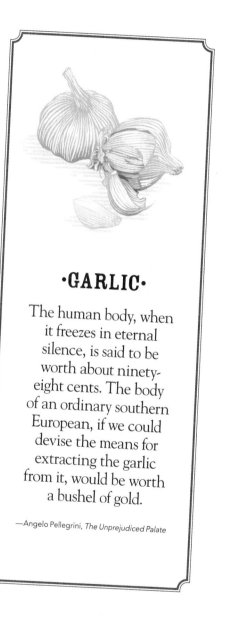

·GARLIC·

The human body, when it freezes in eternal silence, is said to be worth about ninety-eight cents. The body of an ordinary southern European, if we could devise the means for extracting the garlic from it, would be worth a bushel of gold.

—Angelo Pellegrini, *The Unprejudiced Palate*

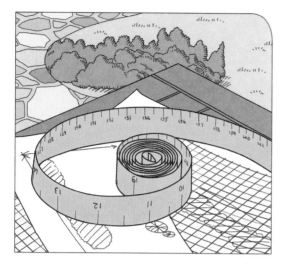

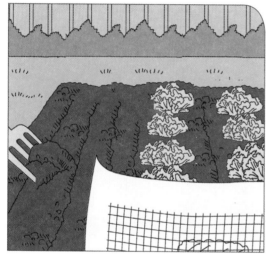

Method: Planning Your Plantings

1 Measure your garden space and plot it on graph paper, using a scale that suits you. A commonly used scale is 1 inch (2.5 cm) of paper to 8 feet (2.5 m) of garden space, but you can adapt it to whatever is easiest for you. Remember, there isn't a law that requires your garden to be square or rectangular. Your garden can be round, curved, or any other shape that fits your landscape or inclination. Does your garden need to be shaped to accommodate trees, a driveway, or flower beds? Show where the sun comes from and which parts are shaded in the morning or afternoon. Make several copies so you can play around with planning your beds on paper.

2 Now you can begin to plan your plantings—in narrow rows or wider beds. Beds in the kitchen garden should allow you to work them from the sides— no more than 3 or 4 feet (0.75 or 1 m) wide for most people. Plot the areas for planting and areas for paths. In a small garden, plant in wide rows or in solid blocks 4–5 feet (1–1.5 m) wide. You must be able to reach the center of each row from either side.

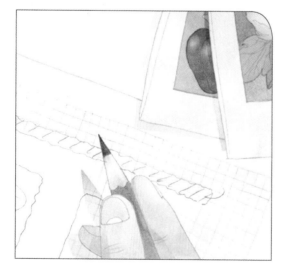

3 Start the plan by sketching in cool-season varieties of vegetables you want to plant. Sketch circles to represent individual transplants, and rows for directly sown seeds. Take care in placing the vegetables. Place taller plants in the north or northeast area of the garden so they won't shade other plants as they grow. If one spot is a little shadier, use it for lettuce or other greens that tend to bolt (go to seed) in the heat of summer. Calculate when these cool-season varieties will mature so that you can replace them with warm-season crops. Draw another plan to indicate the second planting.

BUYING SEEDS AND PLANTS

Seed catalogs are available early in the winter. Ask gardening friends for recommendations of seed companies that have good varieties for your climate. Browse their catalogs to select varieties that appeal to you. Some vegetables will do best if the seeds are started indoors. Consider this if you have adequate indoor light. If not, find out from your local garden supply store which vegetables will be available for purchase as seedlings. Many gardeners get a boost on the season by buying tomato, cucumber, leek, eggplant, cauliflower, pepper, broccoli, cabbage, winter squash, flower, and herb plants. Some vegetables, such as corn, must be started with seed planted in the ground. Some, like lettuce, can be sown directly or bought as started plants and transplanted into the garden.

When it is time to buy vegetable plants, look for those with well-developed leaves, but no fruit. Check to make sure that they are not root-bound (the pot is almost completely filled with roots) and avoid plants that look wilted, spindly, yellowed, or have damaged leaves. Keep the soil in the pots moist until you can plant, and give the plants plenty of light.

WHAT YOU NEED TO KNOW ABOUT SOIL

The ideal garden soil is rich in organic matter, has a neutral or slightly acidic pH, and is well drained. How does your soil measure up? The acidity and amount of nutrients in the soil can be determined by soil tests performed by your state university's Cooperative Extension Service, generally for a small fee. The analysis will tell you the soil pH and how much lime (to raise the pH) or sulfur (to lower pH) it is necessary to add. It should also tell you about the fertility of the soil.

If you decide to improve the soil with a commercial fertilizer (organic or chemical), read the recommendations on the label. Different types of plants need different types of fertilizer. Leafy crops need more nitrogen, while root crops need more phosphorus and potassium. Well-rotted manure and compost increases fertility and improves the texture

The Shape and Size Matter

The size of your garden is up to you. How much space do you have and how much time do you wish to spend gardening?

L-shaped is well suited for a garden that must follow the side of a house or for corner lots.

Terracing is the answer to steep slopes and can be curved to follow natural contours.

Raised beds are the answer to poorly draining soil and are used to extend growing seasons.

of soil. If your soil is either excessively sandy or heavy with clay, you can improve it by working compost, peat humus, peat moss, or other organic material into it. The process of building good soil takes years and is part of the gardening process. During the garden season, you can use organic mulches, such as leaves, sawdust, wood shavings, or spoiled hay, to cover bare soil and prevent weeds. Turn this mulch into the soil at the end of the garden season to improve the texture of the soil and to allow microbes in the soil to begin the process of making the organic materials available as plant food.

Digging In

Stake out your garden plot and dig up the soil using a rotary tiller or hand tools. It is preferable to do this during the fall to expose weed seeds and to give roots and grass a chance to decompose and enrich the soil, but you can also do this in the spring as soon as the soil can be worked. Remove any stones, roots, and debris from the area. Spring is also a good time to test your soil to determine if it needs improvements.

Break up any clumps of soil by spading or tilling a few times before planting, and rake the garden so the soil is smooth. Consider raising the beds—raised beds will be easier to work in, they provide good drainage, and they are attractive. Depending on your budget, you can construct them from treated or plastic lumber, concrete, or plastic forms, or you can simply build them up by mounding the soil.

If you use treated lumber, be sure that it is not old lumber, which may have been treated with arsenic.

Method: Germinating Seeds

If you want to grow your vegetables and herbs from seed, you need to allow them to germinate before planting them in containers.

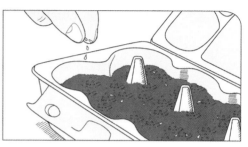

1 Sow the seeds in a plastic tray, pot, or cardboard egg carton filled with compost, or use peat pots from local nursery supply centers.

2 Cover the seeds with ¼–½ inch (5 mm–1 cm) of compost or potting soil. Cover the container with plastic wrap and place in a wam, sunny place. Remove the cover as soon as the seeds germinate. Keep the soil damp but do not overwater. The seedlings need 12–16 hours of light a day. Transplant to larger containers shortly after the first true leaves appear.

PLANTING

Some plants thrive in cool weather and can even survive a frost; others require warm soil. Knowing your planting zone is the easiest way to get a general idea if a plant will survive in your area. (For anyone living in North America, plant hardiness zone maps are available online.) However, other things like sun, shade, soil, and moisture also play important roles, sometimes even more important. Mulching plants with leaves or pine needles can help insulate them from freezing temperatures.

Before planting seedlings, harden them off by exposing them to increasing amounts of direct sun and wind. Make sure they are well watered at this time. To sow seeds, use a rake to mark the exact width of the beds and smooth the soil. Remove any large stones, clumps of soil, and large pieces of organic matter. Sow the seeds by sprinkling them over the bed. Press the seeds into the soil with the back of a hoe. Cover with a layer of moist soil equal to four times the diameter of the seeds. For carrots seeds this means about ¼ inch (5 mm) of soil; for peas this means about 1 inch (2.5 cm) of soil. Once the seeds are covered, tamp down on the entire seedbed with the back of the hoe. If the soil is dry, water lightly; keep the seedbed moist until the seeds have germinated.

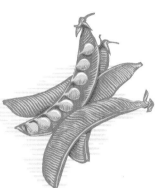

Planting at the Right Times
It's important to understand how vegetables are affected by the season and temperature in which they are planted.

Plant at the Right Time for Your Area

HARDY PLANTS (plant as soon as ground can be worked)	SEMI-HARDY PLANTS (plant 1–2 weeks before average last frost date)	TENDER PLANTS (plant 1 week after date of last frost)	VERY TENDER PLANTS (plant 2 weeks after average date of last frost)
Asparagus	Collards	Celery	Cantaloupe
Beets	Bibb lettuce	Corn	Eggplant
Bok choy	Leaf lettuce	Cucumbers	Lima beans
Broccoli	Swiss chard	Green beans	Peppers
Brussels sprouts	Radishes	New Zealand spinach	Pumpkins
Cabbage	Mustard greens	Summer squash	Watermelon
Carrots	Spinach	Tomatoes	Winter squash
Kale			
Onions			
Parsnips			
Peas			
Rutabagas			
Turnips			

COMPOSTING

Composting is helpful for growing the best and most delicious plants, fruits, and vegetables in your kitchen garden. The process involves allowing plant material to decompose into an earthy, dark, and crumbly substance that will enrich your garden soil. As well as giving you the best start to your garden, composting also takes care of the environment by recycling your yard and kitchen waste. Both practical and responsible, composting is easy to learn.

Making a Compost Pile

To begin, you will need a compost pile or bin. You can use an old container out of sight, or purchase a more visually appealing bin from your local hardware store. Site your compost pile or bin on a level, well-drained, sunny area in the garden, preferably screened from the house. In this position, the pile will be accessible for worms to get in and begin breaking down the compost. The heat from the sun will help to speed up the composting process. The size of your compost pile will depend on available space.

Build up the pile with "greens" such as tea bags, fruit and vegetable peelings, grass clippings, and plant cuttings. These rot fast and provide nitrogen and moisture. You can also compost "browns," such as cardboard egg cartons, fallen leaves, eggshells, and shredded paper. These take longer to break down, but are useful in providing fiber and carbon, as well as air, in the mix.

Check your compost pile regularly. If it gets too dry, add more greens; if it becomes too wet, add more browns. Be

Making It Easy:
Composting

Compost is nature's way of recycling organic material into fertilizer for plants. For the gardener, compost turns a problem (dealing with garden waste) into a solution (creating fertilizer for free). So how do you make compost? With four simple ingredients:

- **Green** Grass clippings, weeds, and kitchen scraps (except meat).

- **Brown** Cardboard egg cartons, fallen leaves, eggshells, shredded paper, straw, hay, wood shavings or chips.

- **Water** Make sure your mixture remains damp.

- **Air** Turn it all every few days to reintroduce oxygen to the pile.

That's all you need. In less than a month, you'll have rich, crumbly, brown compost that you can add to your garden soil, use in containers, or use as mulch. You can make compost anywhere—in a pile in the corner of the garden or in a commercial bin.

Worm Composting Worms can break down material into compost even in very small spaces. Starter kits are available from specialty stores. Red worms or red wrigglers are best because they thrive on kitchen waste.

sure to create air pockets, too, by adding scrunched-up paper or cardboard, and by mixing the compost regularly.

After six to nine months, the compost at the bottom will be dark brown, almost black, with a spongy texture and earthy smell. Spread it on your vegetable beds, or spray as a compost tea, to improve the quality of the soil, retain moisture, and suppress weeds.

How a Compost Pile Works

The waste in a compost pile breaks down into nutritious fertilizer. Initially, microbes start eating the greens. The energy produced as a result increases the temperature of the pile and generates more microbes; then mold starts to appear. Mini-beasts, such as worms, woodlice, and ants, help to break down the greens further. When the greens are broken down, the temperature begins to drop and the fungi get to work on breaking down the browns. Snails, slugs, and beetles also help in this process.

What to Compost

Materials that should go on your compost pile include shrub and lawn clippings, and kitchen wastes, such as fruit and vegetable peels/rinds, tea bags, coffee grounds, and eggshells. Leaves, straw, weeds, wood chips, and sawdust are also good additions to your pile.

What Not to Compost

Some items should never go on your compost pile, especially chemically treated wood products. If you're getting chips or sawdust from a construction site, check the origin of the wood. Never try to compost diseased plants, and under no circumstances add human wastes, meat or bones, pernicious weeds (which can grow in the compost), or waste from pets.

Method: Adjusting the pH of Your Soil

The pH scale, which is used to measure acidity and alkalinity, runs from 0 through 14. A soil with a pH of 3 is very acidic and it is unlikely that plants will grow in it. Each point on the pH scale represents a factor of 10, so a pH of 3 is 10 times more acidic than a pH of 4.

Soils are not homogenous, and the pH can vary considerably in a garden from one spot to another. The pH also changes with the depth of the soil.

The pH of the soil controls the availability of certain nutrients and will affect the health of your plants as well as the rate at which they will grow.

Most soils have a pH ranging from 4–8.5, and most vegetables thrive best between pH 6 and pH 6.8.

Most plants like soil that is neutral to slightly acid, although they do have different needs. Be sure to look carefully at the instructions on any packet of seeds because differing pH conditions will affect them in different ways. For example, potatoes prefer slightly more acidic conditions. In very alkaline soils, potatoes can be affected by bacterial diseases, whereas these bacteria cannot thrive in more acidic soils.

- Correct overly acidic soil by adding lime, which also contributes to the calcium of the soil and improves soil structure.

- Make alkaline soils more acidic by adding aluminum sulfate or powdered sulfur, a slow-acting but long-lasting correcting agent.

Method: Start Your Own Container Plant

Even if you do not have space for lots of beds, most vegetables are easily grown in containers that can be positioned near the kitchen. Container growing also means that you can provide each plant with its own special needs. So herbs native to dry, well-drained soils in the Mediterranean (including sage, thyme, and lavender) can be given a light, open soil, and those requiring heavier soil can be given some with much more body. Group together plants requiring similar conditions and provide the right microclimate.

1 Choose a container, such as a drum, gallon can, tub, or wooden box. The size will vary according to the space available and the plant you are growing.

2 Add about 1 inch (2.5 cm) of coarse gravel to the bottom of the container to provide drainage for the growing plants. Fill the container with lightweight potting soil.

3 Transplant young plants when they have two or three leaves. Make a hole in the soil with your finger, and place the plant in it carefully. Secure in place by firming the soil around the stem.

4 Give the plant water mixed with a little liquid fertilizer. Keep the plants watered every day. Take care not to allow the soil to dry out.

CROPS IN POTS

As long as you have a sunny spot, you can grow vegetables in containers, and any container will do as long as excess water can drain and the container is the right size for the plant—or plants—growing within. The minimum size for most vegetables is 3 gallons (11 L). A box for lettuce and other fast-growing shallow-rooted plants should be at least 8 inches (20 cm) deep. Plants that thrive in containers include lettuce, kale, chard, radishes, tomatoes, peppers, eggplant, and summer squash.

Before filling your containers with packaged potting soil, thoroughly wet the mix and let it sit overnight to absorb the water. Mix in slow-release fertilizer, if needed. If you are using large containers, move them into place before filling; they will be heavy once filled with moist soil. Leave 1–2 inches (2.5–5 cm) of space between the top of the soil and edge of the container to allow you to water without having soil slosh out of the container.

Set your plants into the container about 2 inches (5 cm) away from its edge. Firm down the soil around the roots of the plant.

Water when the soil is dry; sometimes this means twice a day. Fertilize at least once every three weeks.

Next enjoy the harvest!

Trellises Tomato plants yield more fruit on a trellis, which protects the vines.

Stepped Boxes Some plants need more room, so you can buy or make stepped bed containers.

Salad Gardens Lettuce, chives, spinach, and other greens grow well in boxes.

COLD
STORAGE

Your harvest is in and the markets are brimming with
beautiful local produce. Now is the time to start preparing
for winter. Storing fruits and vegetables in a root cellar is the
oldest, fastest, and easiest method of storing food. Root
cellars differ from refrigerators because they provide moist,
cold storage; refrigerators are too dry. Considering the love
and attention your garden received when it was growing, it
is very important to preserve the harvest in a delicious and
healthy state to make sure all your hard work pays off.

While root cellars might be ideal, they are not available
to every budding gardener with a vegetable crop. Luckily,
there are other alternatives. You can use space in a basement
to create the conditions of a root cellar, and storing your
vegetables outside may be a viable option. Depending on the
exact conditions, a layer of leaves might be all you need to
maintain those vegetables in great shape. However, you have
to provide the correct conditions for the produce, and there
are important considerations of temperature, ventilation,
humidity, and drainage (if you are storing your produce
outdoors) that must be followed.

GIVE YOUR PRODUCE
A GOOD PLACE TO REST

Harvesting is always an exciting time, but without proper storage, your crop will lose its freshness and reverse all your hard work. While there are important points to remember when storing, the fundamentals are simple and easy. There's no excuse for letting your beautiful fruits and vegetables go to waste.

GENERAL GUIDELINES FOR COLD STORAGE

Most root vegetables will keep best between 32° and 40° F (0° and 4° C) with 90 to 95 percent humidity, but don't worry about achieving the perfect environment. As long as the temperature where you store your crops is above freezing, cold storage is better than warm-kitchen storage.

Optimizing Your Storage

True, if you can keep the stored crops only moderately cool, they won't last as long, but you still will have extended your garden-vegetable-eating season. Here are some tips to guarantee your success with cold storage.

- Choose varieties of vegetables that are well adapted to storage, as indicated in the seed catalogs.

- Treat all winter-keeping vegetables gently at all stages. Cut, bruised, or diseased vegetables not only spoil more quickly but also encourage spoilage in neighboring foods.

- Leave vegetables in the garden as long as possible, but keep an eye on the weather and rescue them before a frost hits. Low temperatures in fall encourage vegetables to store more sugars and starches than water, making them better keepers.

- Harvest during a dry spell, if possible.

- Pick foods at maturity—neither underdeveloped nor overripe.

- Trim the green tops of all vegetables, leaving a 1-inch (2.5-cm) stub. Take care not to cut the root flesh, and don't cut off root tips, either; any skin break invites spoilage.

- Clean your storage area once a year. Sweep out all debris and scrub all containers with hot, soapy water.

- Don't wash vegetables before packing them away; just gently brush off any large clumps of soil that may cling to them.

- Each vegetable type needs to be stored in a separate container. Containers can be sturdy cardboard boxes, barrels, large plastic bags, or plastic bins.

- Vegetables need to be packed in layers of dried leaves, straw, crumpled or shredded newspapers, or sawdust.

- Some vegetables must be cured in order to keep well. (For more harvesting and handling tips for specific vegetables, see Preserving Vegetables, pages 62–81.)

INDOOR STORAGE

If you have an unheated basement or cellar in your house and you live in a moderate climate, you've got a good start for root storage right there; all you need to do is enclose and insulate the space. If you have a heated basement, you may be able to partition off a room in the northeast corner to make a root cellar. If you have a north- or east-facing hill on your property, you can dig into the slope and line the space with stone or concrete blocks. On flat land you can go straight underground and dig a cavern, insulate and roof it, and then top it with a shed. Many gardeners in the U.S. Midwest build mound-topped underground food closets that double as storm shelters.

Root Cellars

The advantage of root cellars is that you have lots of room and can inspect your produce regularly, removing vegetables as needed.

Conditions Give your cold-storage room both air-intake and air-exhaust pipes so you can chill it by admitting cold night air and by venting warm air (along with ethylene gas given off by some ripening fruits). Good air circulation will help to control

Light and Shade
Sunlight was perfect while your garden was growing, but you don't want the heat of the sun on your harvested crop! Keep vegetables in the shade when storing.

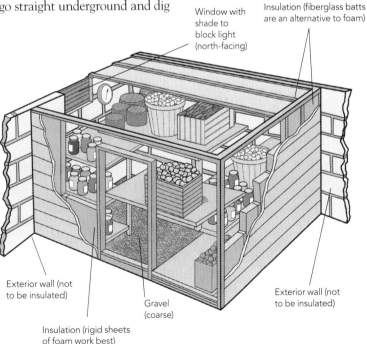

Window with shade to block light (north-facing)

Insulation (fiberglass batts are an alternative to foam)

Exterior wall (not to be insulated)

Gravel (coarse)

Exterior wall (not to be insulated)

Insulation (rigid sheets of foam work best)

Making It Easy:
Cold Storage Outside

The simplest of all cold-storage schemes is to leave some root vegetables right in the garden. An insulating layer of leaf-filled bags or of hay bales settled on top of the row will extend the digging season. Raised-bed gardeners have the advantage here because their well-drained garden soil stays diggable longer. Even after the ground freezes too hard to dig, your winter blanket will help preserve such roots as carrots, salsify, and parsnips until early spring. Mice can be a problem, so you might want to spread a sheet of hardware cloth over the crop before piling on the hay.

the condensation of moisture on the vegetables. Keep the room dark; light encourages sprouting in potatoes. Finally, close all spaces as tightly as you can to keep mice out. This means screening all vent pipes and windows and making sure the door fits tightly. Build shelves to expand the useful space in your cellar. The shelves need to be slatted for good air circulation and built 1–2 inches (2.5–5 cm) from the wall so air can circulate.

Easy Alternatives

If building a root cellar is out of the question, you may still have plenty of cold-storage options.

Basement Stairs In colder climates where the stairs have an outdoor entrance, these can make an excellent alternative root cellar. Install a door at the top of the steps to block off heat from the house, and use the steps as shelves, with the top shelves holding crops that need to be kept coolest (potatoes) and the bottom steps holding vegetables more tolerant of heat (winter squash). Place pans of water on the steps to provide the necessary moisture and replenish the water as needed. In warmer climates you may need to look elsewhere in your house for a suitable area.

More Spaces Where else do you have space that is unheated but stays above freezing?

- An unheated enclosed porch
- A spare bedroom
- A cold attic
- A north-side closet on an exterior wall

OUTDOOR STORAGE

Storing your vegetables outside can be a useful method if you don't have a root cellar or basement. Some vegetables, such as kale, fare best left in the garden. Others can be placed in special in-garden storage areas.

Harvest When Needed

Leave root crops in the ground, but dig them up as early in spring as you can, because the quality of the food is best before new green tops start to sprout. Root vegetables dug in the spring may surprise you; the freezing temperatures convert starches to sugar and often improve flavor!

Kale is a hardy green that can withstand several frosts in the garden. Just brush off the snow and harvest into November or December. Brussels sprouts can withstand a few light frosts, which will add a purple tint to the greenery.

Method: Building Clamps

Clamps are earth-covered mounds that allow you to store vegetables in your garden. Before you start your clamps, be sure to pick a dry, well-drained spot. Because clamps must be emptied once opened in midwinter, you might want to make several small clamps and put a mixture of several kinds of vegetables—beets, carrots, parsnips, potatoes, rutabagas, turnips—in each.

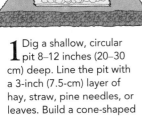

1 Dig a shallow, circular pit 8–12 inches (20–30 cm) deep. Line the pit with a 3-inch (7.5-cm) layer of hay, straw, pine needles, or leaves. Build a cone-shaped pile of produce up to 2 or 3 feet (60 or 90 cm) high in the pit, with alternating layers of root vegetables and straw.

2 Cover the produce with dry leaves, hay, sand, or sawdust. Then add 4 inches (10 cm) of soil, letting the layer below poke out through the top for air.

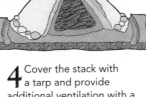

3 Shovel out a narrow drainage channel around the perimeter of the hole. Next place a metal or wood cover over the top to protect the produce from rain and runoff.

4 Cover the stack with a tarp and provide additional ventilation with a wide central opening. Place a metal or plastic rain shield on the top.

Method: Burying Clean Trash Cans

You can bury clean trash cans in the ground and fill them with food—you'll have a secure outside storage area until spring. Barrels and old refrigerators work well, too.

1 Dig a hole wide enough to hold the container and about 10 inches (25 cm) deeper than its height. Toss 3 inches (7.5 cm) of gravel into the hole, settle the container in the space, then pack the space with alternating layers of root vegetables and straw.

2 Stuff more straw into the top 6 inches (15 cm) of the buried food-safe, cover with a board held down with a stone, and layer with another 12 inches (30 cm) of straw or hay topped by a second larger board.

1a Alternatively, you can dig a shallow ditch for the can, about the depth of its radius, and lay it on its side in the ditch. Pack earth around it.

2b Place boards at an angle on top and nail into place.

IDEAL STORAGE CONDITIONS FOR FRUITS AND VEGETABLES

Most fruits and vegetables tend to keep for longer if kept in moist, cool conditions. Some can last for months in ideal conditions. Crops can remain fresh and usable for months in cold storage. However, not all fruits and vegetables have the same ideal storage temperature. It is important to know the various optimum conditions to ensure that your crops stay fresh. For example, potatoes need it damp, while winter squash need dry conditions. You can use the table below as a guide to determine the best conditions for storing different fruits and vegetables.

COLD/VERY DAMP (32°–40° F/0°–4° C and 90–95% relative humidity)	COLD/DAMP (32°–40° F/0°–4° C and 80–90% relative humidity)	COOL/DRY (35°–40° F/2°–4° C and 60–70% relative humidity)	WARM/DRY (50°–60° F/10°–15° C and 60–70% relative humidity)
Beets	Apples	Garlic	Green tomatoes (may be kept up to 70° F [21° C])
Carrots	Cabbage	Green soybeans in the pod	
Celery	Cauliflower (short-term)	Onions	Hot peppers, dried
Celery root	Endive		Pumpkins
Chinese cabbage	Escarole		Sweet potatoes
Horseradish	Grapefruit		Winter squash
Jerusalem artichokes	Grapes		
Kohlrabi	Oranges		
Leeks	Pears		
Parsnips	Potatoes		
Rutabagas	Quince		
Salsify			
Turnips			
Winter radishes			

Wrapping

Fruit stores better when it is wrapped, particularly when stored near vegetables. Wrap the fruits individually in newspaper to prevent them from picking up off-odors.

Troubleshooting Once you have stored your fruit, it is important to check it regularly. One spoiled item can turn the whole crop, so remove it immediately. Rotten fruit indicates poor ventilation.

APPROXIMATE STORAGE TIMES

Use the table (right) as a guide for how long fruits and vegetables can be stored and still stay fresh. Notice that some vegetables can be stored for only a few weeks, as opposed to others, that can keep for up to 6 months!

To get the maximum storage time out of your crops, it is important to prepare them properly. Remember to brush off the fruits and vegetables (although do not wash produce before storage!), removing any that may be bruised or damaged. Also do not pile them high and together in one big container. Try to keep them from touching each other by using several smaller containers. This will lessen the risk of one contaminated batch affecting all the others.

USING STORED FRUITS AND VEGETABLES

Every time you take a fruit or vegetable out of storage, check that it has not been contaminated by mold or fungus. If you find any signs of this, check the rest of the batch and discard as needed. Also, clean the produce thoroughly before using, and do not re-store partially used produce, which is more prone to contamination.

Storing the Right Items Together

Ethylene "producers," fruits that release large amounts of ethylene gas as they ripen, should not be stored with fruits, vegetables, or flowers that are sensitive to this. For example, apples produce a lot of ethylene and will make carrots bitter if the two are stored together.

VEGETABLE	LENGTH OF STORAGE
Beets	4–5 months
Broccoli	1–2 weeks
Brussels sprouts	3–5 weeks
Cabbage	3–4 months
Carrots	4–6 months
Chinese cabbage	1–2 months
Eggplant	1–2 weeks
Jerusalem artichokes	1–2 months
Parsnips	1–2 months
Potatoes	4–6 months
Pumpkins	5–6 months
Radishes	2–3 months
Rutabagas	2–4 months
Tomatoes	1–2 months
Turnips	4–6 months
Winter squash	4–6 months

SOME EXAMPLES OF ETHYLENE EFFECTS

- Toughness in turnips
- Bitterness in carrots and parsnips
- Yellowing of leaves in broccoli, cabbage, and cauliflower
- Early softening of squash
- Discoloration of sweet potatoes
- Sprouting of potatoes

·TOMATO·

Shall I not have intelligence with the earth? Am I not partly leaves and vegetable mold myself?

—Henry David Thoreau

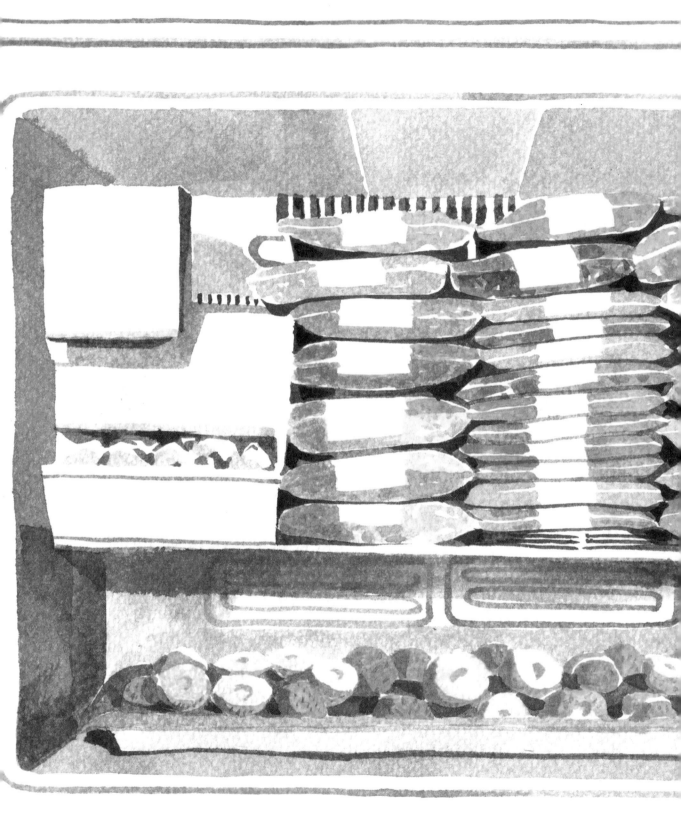

FREEZING

Freezing is an easy way to preserve. This process applies to the widest range of fruits and vegetables, and it is best for maintaining flavor, texture, and nutritional value. Freezing is also fast and easy. It can be done in small batches, so there is little stress, specialized equipment, or space required. Just as with any preserving method, there are some procedures to follow before you finally freeze your produce. For example, some items may need blanching or placing in syrup. You will need to know what type of containers are best, and also the techniques for packing that will ensure your fruit and vegetables stay tasty.

There are some extremely easy freezing methods, but sometimes the quick option will result in produce suitable for pies and preserves rather than eating thawed. If you have the time, consider freezing your excess produce as ready-made sauces, soups, or pie fillings. The cooking process creates an ideal fruit or vegetable dish for freezing, and having ready-made items already stored will save you time at a later date.

FREEZING THE FRUITS (AND VEGETABLES) OF YOUR LABOR

Select fruits and vegetables for freezing that are at their peak of flavor and texture. If possible, harvest in the cool part of the morning and process as quickly as possible. If you can't freeze immediately, immerse the fruits or vegetables in very cold water or refrigerate in shallow trays to preserve quality and nutrients. To prepare the produce for freezing, peel and chop as desired. See Preserving Vegetables (pages 62–81) and Preserving Fruit (pages 82–93) for information on preserving specific vegetables and fruits.

CONTAINERS

You'll need to stock up on freezer containers that are moisture- and vapor-proof to maintain the best quality. Your choices range from rigid plastic containers to plastic-film bags made especially for freezing. Collapsible cardboard freezer boxes can be used as an outer covering for plastic bags to protect them against tearing and for easy stacking in the freezer. Don't use thin plastic sandwich bags or recycled bread wrappers. Label your containers with a permanent marker for easy retrieval.

"Freeze-and-cook" or "boilable" bags are expensive but very convenient. They are designed to hold frozen vegetables and to cook these same vegetables, still in the bag, resulting in a very high-quality product. They come in 1½-pint (750-ml) and quart (1-L) sizes and also as large rolls of plastic so that they can be made to the size desired. A heat sealer is necessary for closing these bags.

Freezer Containers Your produce should always be filled to the top and sealed properly to prevent freezer burn.

FREEZING VEGETABLES

Vegetables will retain the best quality if they are blanched before they are frozen (see page 34). Then pack them for freezing using the dry pack or tray pack method.

Packing Methods

Tray packing gives you good flexibility in the way you can use the vegetables, but it is a little more tricky than dry packing in batches. Choose whichever method suits you best.

Dry Pack Blanch the vegetables for the length of time specified on page 81, drain well, dry thoroughly, and pack into freezer containers or freezer bags. For the best quality, the vegetables need to be as dry as possible and packed tightly to cut down on the amount of air in the container.

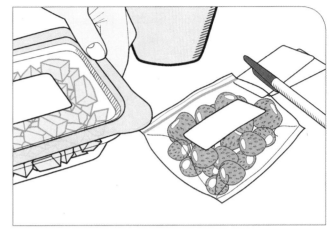

Tray Pack Blanch and dry the vegetables as above, then spread the vegetables in a single layer on a tray or baking sheet and freeze. As soon as the vegetables are frozen (it will take about 1 hour), pack them into freezer bags or containers. The advantage of this method is that you will be able to pour out as much of the frozen vegetable as you want, then return the rest of the bag to the freezer. Tray packing is particularly good for peas, corn, and beans. Items that are tray packed will last well in the freezer for about 12 months.

Packing If you are packing the vegetables in freezer bags, press air out of the unfilled part of the bag before sealing.

Getting the Best Results

When choosing vegetables to freeze, select items that have reached their peaks of flavor and texture. One way to ensure optimum freshness is to harvest the vegetables in the cool of the morning and then process them for storage as quickly as possible. If you cannot freeze them right away, submerge the vegetables in very cold water or refrigerate in shallow trays to preserve their quality and nutrients.

THAWING AND USING

With a few exceptions, you should not thaw frozen vegetables before cooking. Corn should be thawed, and greens, broccoli, and asparagus cook best if thawed a little and then broken into pieces. If you are thawing vegetables, use the refrigerator or place them under cold running water rather than thawing at room temperature. Prepare only enough frozen vegetables for the meal that will be eaten that day. You should not refreeze vegetables that have been cooked from frozen.

> **EQUIPMENT AND SUPPLIES**
> - Large pot—minimum capacity of 2 gallons (7.5 L)
> - Wire basket, colander, or net bag for blanching
> - Hot pads
> - Timer or a clock with a second hand
> - Large pans or bowls for cooling
> - Ice for cooling
> - Kitchen towels or salad spinner
> - Plastic freezer bags or other containers
> - Tray or baking sheet (optional)

Method: Blanching before Freezing

Blanching fixes the color and texture of vegetables by killing bacteria and stopping enzyme action. The more delicate the vegetable, the briefer the blanching time.

You can blanch in boiling water or by steaming. You can use the same blanching water two or three times. Change the water if it becomes cloudy and add more as needed. Work with no more than 1 pound (450 g) of vegetables at a time; otherwise, the vegetables may not blanch evenly. Microwave blanching isn't recommended because microwaves cook unevenly.

1 For boiling-water blanching, bring 4 quarts (3 L) water to a rolling boil for each pound (450 g) of vegetables (leafy greens need 2 gallons [7.5 L] water per pound [450 g]). For steam blanching, bring a few inches (several centimeters) of water to a boil.

2 Immerse a wire basket or mesh bag containing vegetables directly in the boiling water or in the steam above the boiling water.

3 Cover the pot and begin counting the blanching time (see chart on page 81) from the time the vegetables were placed in the water or steam.

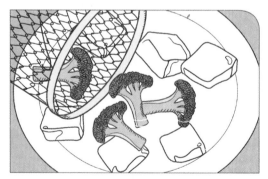

4 Lift the basket or bag out of the water or steam and immediately plunge the vegetables into a basin of ice water. When the vegetables are cold, drain them thoroughly.

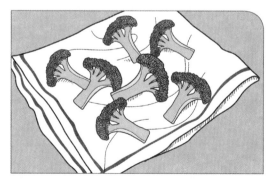

5 Spread the vegetables out on towels on the kitchen counter and let dry, or spin dry in a salad spinner, working with small quantities at a time. Pack the vegetables using one of the methods described on page 33.

FREEZING FRUITS

There are three ways to prepare fruit for freezing: sprinkled with sugar (sugar pack), floating in a sugar syrup (syrup pack), and tray freezing. Most frozen fruits maintain high quality for 8–12 months, but unsweetened fruits lose their color and quality faster than those packed in sugar or sugar syrups.

Method: Preparing Fruit for Freezing

1 Wash and cut away poor-quality parts. Then stem, peel, pit, slice, or chop as necessary. See tips in Preserving Fruit, pages 82–93.

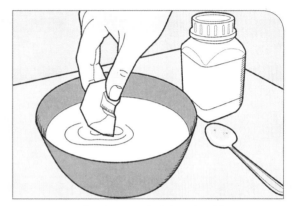

2 To prevent discoloration, dip light-colored fruits in an ascorbic acid solution. Use 1 teaspoon (5 ml) ascorbic acid (available at drugstores and supermarkets) per 2 cups (0.5 L) water.

3 Add sugar or sugar syrup as described on page 36. Pack in containers using one of the methods described on page 33 and freeze.

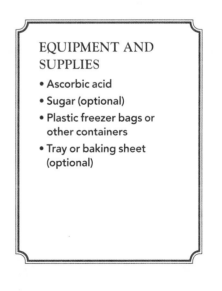

EQUIPMENT AND SUPPLIES
- Ascorbic acid
- Sugar (optional)
- Plastic freezer bags or other containers
- Tray or baking sheet (optional)

Packing Techniques

Freezing fruit is an easy, inexpensive way of preserving your precious harvest, but there are different methods to try.

Sugar Pack Sprinkle the required amount of sugar over the fruit. Gently stir until the pieces are coated with sugar and juice, then pack in freezer containers and freeze.

Syrup Pack Refer to the chart below, and dissolve the required amount of sugar in lukewarm water. You will need about 1½ cups (350 ml) of syrup for every 4 cups (600 g) of fruit. Stir the mixture and let stand until the solution is clear. Sugar syrup can be kept for up to 2 days in the refrigerator. Immerse the fruit in the syrup, pack into containers, and freeze.

Tray Freeze This is an easy method for berries. Simply spread the fruit in a single layer on a tray and freeze. Once frozen, transfer to freezer containers or plastic bags.

Making Sugar Syrups for Freezing Fruit

When packed with sugar or sugar syrup, fruits generally retain best color and quality (see page 35 for advice on preventing discoloration), but heavy syrups may be too sweet and overpower more delicate fruits. Sugar syrup for freezing fruit is made using lukewarm water (see page 93 for syrups used for canning, which are made using boiling water).

TYPE OF SYRUP	GRANULATED SUGAR	WATER	SYRUP YIELD
Light	2 cups (500 g)	4 cups (950 ml)	5 cups (1.2 L)
Medium	3 cups (750 g)	4 cups (950 ml)	5½ cups (1.3 L)
Heavy	4¾ cups (1.1 kg)	4 cups (950 ml)	6½ cups (1.5 L)

THAWING AND USING

Thaw fruit at room temperature in its original package. If you need to defrost in a hurry, submerge the container in cool or lukewarm water or follow microwave defrosting instructions. Serve as soon as possible, preferably while a few ice crystals remain. Most fruits can be frozen for at least 12 months. Longer storage will not make the food inedible, but the decrease in quality will be very noticeable.

Fruits with a Shorter Lifespan

Although most produce will freeze perfectly well for up to one year, some fruits can pass their best much quicker. Citrus fruits, such as oranges, lemons, limes, and grapefruit, freeze well but may only keep their strong flavors for 4–6 months. Make sure you put labels and dates on all your produce when freezing, and then you can make sure it is all consumed when at its most flavorful.

NUTRITION OF FROZEN FRUIT AND VEGETABLES

Vegetables and fruits that are frozen when fresh will retain much of their nutritional value. Vitamin B_6, for example, is found in significant quantities in peas and carrots, both of which freeze well.

Most Nutritious Ways to Use Frozen Produce

Don't boil vegetables. Try to think of delicious ways to serve fruit without cooking or baking them. For example:

Smoothies Instead of ice, use frozen fruit to add a cold and chunky crunch to your beverage. The ingredients will be as healthy as physically possible.

Stir-fries By adding your vegetables to oil rather than boiling water, you seal in the vitamins and minerals, and almost any vegetable combination can make a delicious stir-fry.

·STRAWBERRIES·

Strawberries are the angels of the earth, innocent and sweet with green leafy wings reaching heavenward.

—Jasmine Heiler

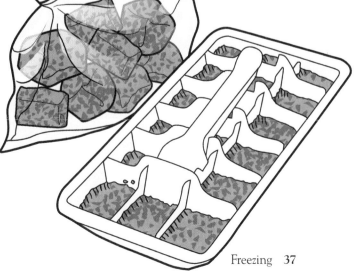

Frozen Herbs Freezing your herbs will preserve their potent flavors and aromas.

FREEZING HERBS

Place chopped herbs in ice-cube trays, pour boiling water over them, and freeze. Once solid, pop out the cubes and store in a freezer bag until you're ready to use them. Or mix chopped fresh herbs with butter and freeze as herb butters.

Freezer Salsa

This uncooked salsa needs to be defrosted in a colander over a bowl. Return just enough drained liquid to the salsa to create a good consistency.

1 onion, peeled and
   finely chopped

8–10 tomatoes, peeled and
   finely chopped

2 cloves garlic, crushed

2 fresh red or green chiles, finely
   chopped

Fresh cilantro to taste

Combine all of the ingredients, then transfer to freezer containers in suitable portion sizes.

Freezer Pesto

Keeping a supply of classic pesto in the freezer means you can whip up a hearty pasta meal in no time.

Handful fresh basil leaves

Handful pine nuts

5–6 tablespoons (75–85 ml)
   olive oil

Salt and black pepper

Blend all ingredients in a food processor.

Freeze pesto in small, portion-size containers, topped off with a layer of olive oil to exclude air and prevent discoloration.

Freezer Tomato Sauce

This meatless cooked tomato sauce can be defrosted and combined with your choice of vegetables, herbs, and/or meat to accompany your favorite pasta.

1 onion, peeled and finely chopped

2 cloves garlic, crushed

3 tablespoons (45 ml) olive oil

5 cups (800 g) tomatoes,
    finely chopped

Salt and black pepper
2–3 tablespoons chopped fresh
    basil or oregano

Heat the oil in a large frying pan. Add the onion and garlic and sauté until soft. Add the tomatoes and cook over a gentle heat for 15 minutes until most of the liquid has evaporated. Add salt, pepper, and fresh herbs to taste. Allow to cool and transfer to freezer containers. Defrost before use.

Frozen Apple Pie Filling

Thawing is not necessary with frozen apple pie filling.

5½ cups (1 kg) cooking apples,
    peeled, cored, and sliced

½ cup (85 g) granulated sugar

2–3 tablespoons white flour

1 teaspoon (5 ml) ground
    cinnamon

Toss the apple slices with the sugar, flour, cinnamon and freeze in a pie pan. Once frozen, slip out of pie pan, wrap well in plastic wrap and freezer paper, and return to freezer.

When ready to bake, slip frozen apples into prepared pie shell and bake.

CANNING

There are two types of canning methods: boiling-water bath canning for high-acid foods (fruit, jams, pickles, and tomatoes) and pressure-canning for low-acid foods (most vegetables). Before committing to either type of canning, ask yourself what you want to can. While it may be convenient to have canned peas on hand, you may prefer the taste of frozen peas.

On the other hand, nothing beats the convenience of opening a jar of tomatoes ready for cooking or applesauce ready for eating. Ultimately you want to maximize the life and flavor of your fruit and vegetables, and preserving them yourself is one way to make sure your pantry is stocked with only the foods you really want to eat. Follow the handy hints in this chapter to get the best out of your produce.

CANNING BASICS FOR PRESERVING FOOD

Canning may seem scary, but it is really quite simple, as long as you follow the guidelines in this chapter. After a few batches, you will recognize how easy and rewarding canning can be.

GENERAL GUIDELINES FOR CANNING

Foods can be packed into canning jars cooked or uncooked. Cooked food goes in hot (hot-pack), and raw food goes into the jars unheated (raw-pack). Most hot-packed foods are cooked in water, a juice, or syrup. Tomatoes and some fruits are often cooked in their own juices. Raw-packed foods are packed in a sugar syrup, fruit juice, or vinegar brine. The advantage of raw-packed foods is that the process is quicker. The advantages of hot-packed foods are that the foods are less likely to shrink and float in the cooking liquid, more food can be packed in each jar, and it looks better.

Canning Equipment

Beyond the basic kitchen equipment you already have, almost everything you will need for canning is readily available at supermarkets and hardware stores.

Boiling-water Bath Canner Use this for processing fruits, pickles, and high-acid vegetables only. The canner is basically a large pot that comes with a wire rack to hold canning jars.

Pressure Canner This specially made heavy pot has a lid that can be closed to prevent steam from escaping. The lid is fitted with a petcock, which is a vent that can open and close to allow air and steam to escape from the canner. It also has a dial- or weighted-pressure gauge to register

---

CANNING SAFETY

Never eat home-canned food you think may be spoiled! A bulging lid or leaking jar is a sign of spoilage. When you open the jar, there should be no spurting or bubbling liquid, and no mold or off-odors. Spoiled foods should be discarded where they will not be eaten by humans or pets.

---

the pressure inside the canner. Pressure canners come deep enough for one layer of 1-quart (1-L) or smaller-sized jars, or deep enough for two layers of 1-pint (475-ml) or smaller-sized jars.

Getting Ready

Buying your canning equipment can become daunting when confronted with the different options. Do you want a large granite water bath or a small stainless-steel pressure canner? To make everything from preserves to pickles, whole canned tomatoes to chutneys, you cannot go wrong with a boiling-water bath. A tall pressure canner can also be used in the place of a boiling-water bath canner, as long as there is enough space above the jars to allow for 1 inch of boiling water above the lids. To use a pressure canner as a boiling-water bath, place the lid loosely on the canner, but do not fasten it. Leave the vent wide open so that steam escapes and pressure does not build.

Kits If unsure about the different equipment necessary for canning, you can purchase a kit from many cooking stores or from an online retailer. They are aimed at the beginner market and usually include the essential items, such as a pressure-canner, recipe book, timer, funnel, spatula, jar wrench, and tongs. The drawback, however, is that you may already have several of these items, and you do not want to spend money on unnecessary equipment.

Accessories As well as the basics, online stores and cooking outlets will try to sell you a host of products and accessories for canning. It would be prudent not to buy anything until you know you need it.

Watch Out for
- Timing and pressures will vary for high altitudes.
- Do not let the pressure drop during pressure canning—increase the heat to restore lost pressure.

·PICKLES·

Life. A spiritual pickle preserving the body from decay.

— Ambrose Bierce

Canning Equipment

In addition to the equipment listed here, a number of other home-canning accessories, such as corn cutters, apple slicers, decorative labels, and special canning spoons, are available. Some of these items may simplify the process but are not essential.

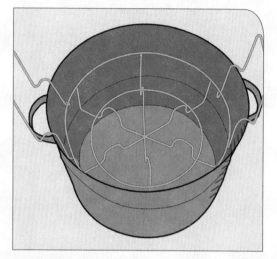

Choosing a canner A plain stainless-steel canner with a jar rack is good for all basic canning requirements.

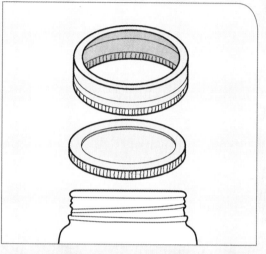

Two-piece lids A flat disk, called a dome lid, sits on top of the jar, and a screwband holds it in place. The lid cannot be reused, but undamaged screwbands can be used again.

Canning jars Made from tempered glass in ½-pint (250-ml), pint (475-ml), quart (1-L), and 2-quart (2-L) sizes, designed to be reusable. (Do not use jars in which you bought commercially prepared sauce or jam because the glass may not be strong enough.)

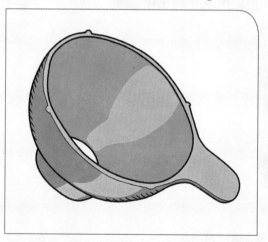

Wide-mouth funnel To help pack small food items into canning jars.

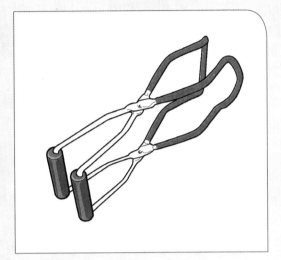

Jar lifter For easy removal of hot jars from canner.

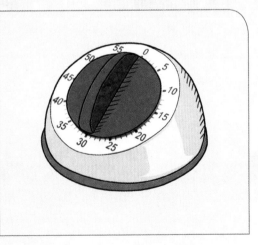

Plastic knife, spatula, or chopstick For removing air bubbles from the jars.

Clean cloths For wiping jar rims and general cleanup.

Timer or clock To indicate end of processing time.

Method: Boiling-Water Bath

Boiling-water bath canning is a safe way to preserve jams, jellies, fruit in syrup, pickles, and tomatoes. The boiling-water bath heats the contents of the jar sufficiently to kill bacteria, molds, and other spoilage organisms. During processing, air is forced out of the jars, leaving a vacuum sealed by the lid. As long as the jars remain airtight, the vacuum protects the food inside from harmful organisms.

1 Prepare the food according to the recipe. For details on tomatoes, see pages 71–72. For fruit, see Preserving Fruit, pages 82–93.

2 Prepare the lids and screwbands according to the manufacturer's directions. Or put them in a pan of water and bring the water just to a boil. Turn off the heat but keep the lids and screwbands in the hot water for at least 10 minutes. Do not remove them until you are ready to put them on the jars.

3 Prepare the jars. You do not have to sterilize jars used for food processed for at least 10 minutes. Simply wash them in soapy water or in a dishwasher, then rinse thoroughly to remove all traces of soap. When you are processing for less than 10 minutes, sterilize the clean jars by submerging them in a canner filled with hot (not boiling) water, making sure the water rises 1 inch (2.5 cm) above the jar top. At sea level, boil the jars for 10 minutes; at higher elevations, boil for an additional minute for every 1,000 feet (300 m) of elevation. Alternatively, you can use the sterilizing cycle available on many dishwashers.

4 Fill the jars, leaving a ½-inch (1-cm) headspace or the headspace indicated in your recipe. Wipe away any drips on the rims of the jars. If bubbles appear as you fill the jars, run a clean spatula or chopstick inside the jar to release them. Do not stir—this could create more bubbles.

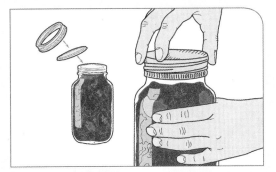

5 Place the lids on top and secure with a screwband, tightening it so it grips. Do not exert extra pressure or make it extremely tight. Load the jars into the rack.

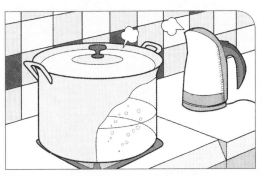

6 Fill the canner half full with water and preheat to about 180° F (80° C). Pour water into a kettle and bring it to a boil.

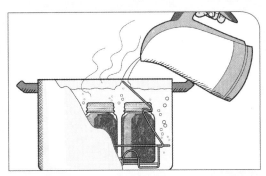

7 Lift the rack by its handles and set it in the canner. If necessary, add more boiling water from the kettle to bring the water level to 1 inch (2.5 cm) above the jars.

8 Turn the heat as high as possible and wait until the water is boiling vigorously. Cover the canner with the lid. Reduce the heat to maintain a moderate boil. As soon as you have covered the canner, set a timer for the recommended processing time. If you live at a high elevation, increase the processing time as necessary, using the explanation on page 50.

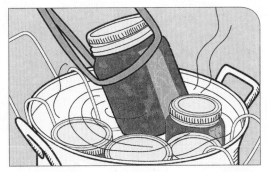

9 When the jars have boiled for the recommended time, remove them from the canner using a jar lifter. Set them on towels, placing them at least 1 inch (2.5 cm) apart.

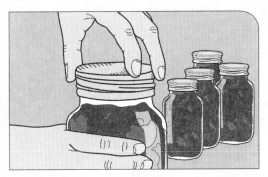

10 Establish that you have a good seal (see page 50). Store the jars in a cool, dry place.

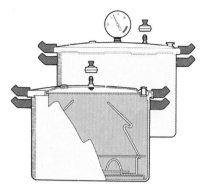

Pressure Canners These work by using steam to push out all the air, creating a much higher temperature than open-water baths.

Making It Easy:
Sharing the Canning

Canning doesn't lend itself to shortcuts. The best way to lighten the workload is to share it. Gather together some like-minded friends and work assembly-line fashion to keep batch after batch of food going in and out of the canner(s). Look into "borrowing" a commercial kitchen—at a school, community center, or restaurant on its day off—to give you enough elbow room to work comfortably. And have fun!

Method: Pressure-Canning

Pressure-canning is used for low-acid foods, including most vegetables and meat.

Modern pressure-canners are lightweight thin-walled kettles; most have turn-on lids fitted with gaskets. They all have removable racks, an automatic vent/cover lock, a vent port (steam vent), and a safety fuse.

The pressure canner may have a dial gauge for indicating the pressure, or a weighted gauge for indicating and regulating the pressure. Read your manufacturer's directions to know how to assemble your canner and how a particular weighted gauge should rock or jiggle.

1 Prepare the food in the jars. To raw-pack, put uncooked food in jars and pour boiling water, juice, or syrup over the food, leaving the proper amount of headspace. To hot-pack, pack in the hot food and cover with boiling cooking liquid, leaving the proper amount of headspace.

2 Prepare the canner by filling with 2–3 inches (5–7.5 cm) of water. For hot-packed foods, bring the water to 180° F (80° C), but be careful not to boil the water or heat it long enough for the depth to decrease. For raw-packed foods, bring the water to 140° F (60° C).

3 Place the filled jars, fitted with lids, on the jar rack in the canner, using a jar lifter. Fasten the canner lid securely. Leave the weight off the vent port or open the petcock (vent).

4 Turn the heat setting to its highest position. Heat until the water boils and steam flows freely in a funnel shape from the open vent port or petcock. While maintaining the high heat setting, let the steam exhaust continuously for 10 minutes.

5 Place the counterweight or weighted gauge on the vent port, or close the petcock (vent). The canner will pressurize in the next 3–10 minutes. Start timing when the pressure reading on the dial gauge indicates that the recommended pressure has been reached or, for canners without dial gauges, when the weighted gauge begins to jiggle or rock as the manufacturer describes. Regulate the heat under the canner to maintain a steady pressure at or slightly above the correct gauge pressure. If at any time the pressure goes below the recommended amount, bring the canner back to pressure and begin timing the process over from the beginning (using the total original process time).

WHAT IS HEADSPACE?

Headspace is the distance between the top of the food or its liquid and the top of the jar. Leave too much headspace, and a vacuum seal might not form. Leave too little, and the food could boil out of the jar, leaving debris on the rim and preventing a seal.

6 When the proper amount of time has elapsed, turn off the heat and let the canner cool down naturally. While it is cooling, it is also depressurizing.

7 When the canner is completely depressurized, remove the weight from the vent port or open the petcock (vent). Wait 10 minutes; then unfasten the lid and remove it carefully. Lift the lid with the underside away from you so that the steam coming out of the canner does not burn your face.

Continued on page 50

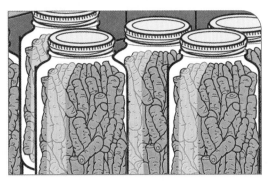

8 Using a jar lifter, remove the jars one at a time and place on a towel, leaving at least 1 inch (2.5 cm) of space between the jars during cooling.

9 Let the jars sit undisturbed while they cool, for 12–24 hours.

ADJUSTING CANNING TIMES FOR ALTITUDE

At sea level, water boils at 212° F (100° C). At higher elevations, it boils at lower temperatures; therefore, in these regions, foods must be processed for longer to ensure that harmful organisms are destroyed. Add 1 minute for every 1,000 feet (300 m) above sea level when processing foods that require less than 20 minutes in the boiling-water bath. Add 2 minutes for every 1,000 feet (300 m) for foods that must be processed for more than 20 minutes.

TESTING FOR A SEAL

After a jar has been processed in a boiling-water bath or pressure canner, it should be sealed. If the seal is faulty, the food inside the jar is not spoiled, but it won't keep long. Store unsealed jars in the refrigerator and use within a week.

To test for a seal:

- Look at the middle of the lid; it should be slightly concave.

- Press the center hard with your thumb; if it does not move downward or "give," it is sealed.

- Remove the screwband and hold the jar by the lid; it should not release the jar.

PROCESSING TIMES FOR LOW-ACID FOODS USING A PRESSURE CANNER (240°F [116°C] AT 10 POUNDS [4.5 KG] OF PRESSURE)

FOOD VEGETABLE	TIME FOR PINTS (mins)	TIME FOR QUARTS (mins)
Asparagus (hot/raw pack)	30	40
Beets (hot pack)	30	35
Carrots (hot/raw pack)	25	30
Corn, cream style (hot pack)	85	Not recommended
Corn, cream style (raw pack)	95	Not recommended
Corn, whole kernel (hot/raw pack)	55	85
Garden peas (hot/raw pack)	40	40
Greens (hot pack)	70	90
Potatoes (hot pack)	35	40
Sweet potatoes, dry (hot pack)	65	95
Sweet potatoes, wet (hot pack)	55	90
Lima beans (hot/raw pack)	40	50
Snap beans (hot/raw pack)	20	25
Okra (hot pack)	25	40
Summer squash (hot pack)	30	40
Summer squash (raw pack)	25	30
Winter squash (hot pack)	55	90
Vegetable soup (hot pack)	Time depends on vegetable requiring the longest processing time.	

Note: Extend processing time one additional minute for each 1,000 feet (300 meters) above sea level.

DRYING

Drying is one of the oldest methods of preserving food. Many fruits and vegetables were originally dried by the sun—sun-dried tomatoes are one popular and delicious example. By removing the moisture, drying is a safe way to preserve your harvest because it prevents the growth of bacteria. It also makes the flavors stronger, showing you an entirely different side of your kitchen garden crop. Dried vegetables are delicious additions to any meal, particularly Mediterranean recipes, and dried fruit is great for a tasty and healthy snack. While this process is both safe and productive, it does mean your produce will lose some of its nutritional value. Sun-dried tomatoes are wonderful, but eating them will not give you the same level of vitamin C that fresh tomatoes will.

Drying will require some special equipment, but this can range from a conventional oven to a variety of dehydrators of different types and prices, or even from your own homemade solar dryer to the traditional basket in the sun. As usual, there is some preparation with this technique, and it can be difficult to know when your produce is done. Persevere—the results are always worth the time.

DRYING FOOD AT HOME

Drying preserves food by removing the moisture upon which food-spoiling bacteria, yeast, and mold depend. Drying also slows down the action of enzymes (naturally occurring substances that cause foods to ripen). Because drying removes moisture, the food shrinks, becomes lighter in weight, and is easier to store. When you want to use dried foods, you can either snack on them directly (dried fruit and beef jerky), or you can add back the water and cook as you would fresh food. Stored in a cool, dark spot, dried food will keep anywhere from several months to two years.

PREPARING FOODS FOR DRYING

It is very simple to prepare fruits and vegetables for drying. Observing the correct method will ensure that your food dries properly and without spoiling.

Fruits

To prepare fruit for drying, first wash and peel the fruit. Cut in half and core, if needed. Slice, if desired. Thin, uniform, peeled slices dry the fastest. Apples can be cored and sliced in rings, wedges, or chips. Bananas can be sliced in coins, chips, or sticks. Fruits dried whole take the longest to dry.

Many light-colored fruits, such as apples, darken rapidly when cut and exposed to air, but you can dip the fruit in an ascorbic acid (vitamin C) solution to prevent browning. Ascorbic acid is available in powdered or tablet form from drugstores and grocery stores. Mix 1 teaspoon (5 g) powdered ascorbic acid (or 3,000 mg of ascorbic acid tablets, crushed) in 2 cups (500 ml) water. Put the fruit in the solution for 3–5 minutes. Remove the fruit and drain well. Spray the dryer trays with nonstick cooking spray to prevent sticking, and place the fruit in a single layer on the trays. The pieces should not touch or overlap.

Sun-Dried Tomatoes
Perfect as antipasti or added to meals, homemade sun-dried tomatoes are always delicious.

Determining Dryness Dry fruit until it is leather-hard but not sticky or tacky. To test for dryness, cut several cooled pieces in half. There should be no visible moisture, and you should not be able to squeeze any moisture from the fruit. Berries should be dried until they rattle when shaken. After drying, cool the fruit for 30–60 minutes. Then condition (see below) before packing away.

Conditioning Fruit Condition the fruit to equalize the moisture among the pieces and reduce the risk of mold growth. To condition the fruit, loosely pack the dried fruit in plastic or glass jars. Seal the containers and let them stand for 7–10 days, shaking the jars daily to separate the pieces and check for moisture condensation. If condensation develops in the jar, return the fruit to the dehydrator for more drying. After conditioning, package and store the fruit.

Vegetables

To prepare vegetables for drying, wash in cool water. Trim, peel, cut, slice, or shred vegetables as desired. Remove any fibrous or woody portions, as well as any decayed and bruised areas. Keep pieces uniform in size so they will dry at the same rate.

Method: Blanching before Drying

Briefly cooking the vegetables (blanching) is necessary for preparing vegetables for drying. Blanching stops the enzyme action that could cause loss of color and flavor during drying and storage. It also shortens the drying and rehydration time by relaxing the tissue walls so moisture can escape and later reenter more rapidly. Blanching can be done in boiling water or by steam.

1 Bring 4 quarts (4 L) water to a rolling boil for each pound (450 g) of vegetables (leafy greens need 2 gallons [7.5 L] per pound [450 g]). For steam blanching, bring a few inches of water to a boil.

2 Immerse a wire basket or mesh bag containing vegetables directly in the boiling water or in the steam above.

3 Cover the pot and begin counting the blanching time from the time the vegetables were placed in the water or steam. For times for specific vegetables, see page 81.

4 Lift the basket out of the water or steam and immediately plunge the vegetables into a basin of ice water. When the vegetables are cold, drain and arrange them on the drying trays.

Determining Dryness Vegetables should be dried until they are brittle. At this stage, they should contain about 10 percent moisture. Because they are so dry, they do not need conditioning like fruits.

DRYING METHODS

Depending on whom you talk to, you come across a host of different methods, temperatures, and lengths of time. This is because the process for drying produce is not an exact science like canning or freezing. Elements such as even temperature and air flow can be unpredictable and alter your outcome slightly, so exercise a trial-and-error approach to find what suits you, your climate, and your budget best. Whatever method you use, it is important to remove enough moisture from the final product so that organisms cannot grow and spoil the food.

Outdoors

A hot, breezy climate with a minimum daytime temperature of 85°F (30° C) is ideal for drying fruit outdoors in the sun. But if the temperature is too low, or the humidity too high, the food may spoil before it is fully dried. The USDA (U.S. Department of Agriculture or Agriculture and Agri-Food in Canada) doesn't recommend drying meat and vegetables outdoors because they are too prone to spoilage.

Equipment Unless you have ready access to woven baskets, you'll probably want to fashion some sort of screened tray. Nylon screening is great. Avoid galvanized metal screens or aluminum or copper screens, which can impart flavors or even potentially toxic salts to the food. Top-quality food-drying screens are made from food-safe plastic screening and are available online.

Cover the trays with cheesecloth or nylon netting to help protect the fruit from birds and insects. Direct sunlight destroys some of the more fragile vitamins and enzymes, and fades the color of the food. You will have better results if you can shade the foods with a dark sheet of cloth or metal. Indoors, it is easy to use screened trays placed on chairs or sawhorses. No additional equipment is needed.

Vine Drying Another method of drying outdoors is vine drying. To dry beans (navy, kidney, butter, black, great northern, lima, lentils, and soybeans), leave bean pods on the vine in the garden until the beans inside rattle. When the vines and pods are dry and shriveled, pick the beans and shell them. No pretreatment is necessary. If the beans are still moist, the drying

Making It Easy:
Low-Tech Dryers

If you want to go really low-tech and you have the climate to make it possible, dry food by draping it over branches or spreading it on wide shallow baskets on a roof. Alternatively, thread pieces of food on a cord or stick and hang it over a fire, wood stove, or from the rafters. Bundle herbs and suspend them from doorknobs or nails in rooms with good ventilation. You can also place screen doors across chairs, or use sheets hung between clotheslines, whether outside, in the attic, or in an upstairs room with screened windows wide open.

process is not complete, and the beans will mold if not more thoroughly dried. If needed, drying can be completed in the sun, the oven, or a dehydrator.

Conventional Ovens

Air circulation in a conventional oven tends to be poor, even with the oven door propped open with a fan placed nearby to improve ventilation, so results can be uneven. Also the process ties up the oven for a long time. It takes about twice as long to dry food in an oven than it does in a dehydrator, so it is not particularly energy-efficient. On the other hand, this method requires no new equipment and can be done in any climate.

Equipment To use an oven to dehydrate food, you must be able to set the oven to 140° F (60° C). At higher temperatures, the food cooks rather than dries. Drying racks should be 3–4 inches (7.5–10 cm) shorter than the oven from front to back. Cake-cooling racks placed on top of cookie sheets work well for some foods. The oven racks, holding the trays, should be 2–3 inches (5–7.5 cm) apart for air circulation.

Electric Dehydrators

This appliance gives excellent and consistent results. The only drawbacks are the cost of buying and running the appliance, the limited amount of food that can be dried at one time in most home models, and the storage space the appliance requires when not in use.

·TOMATOES·

A world without tomatoes is like a string quartet without violins.

—Laurie Colwin

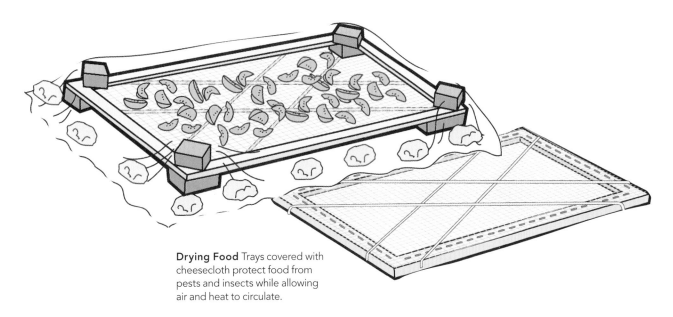

Drying Food Trays covered with cheesecloth protect food from pests and insects while allowing air and heat to circulate.

Equipment A food dehydrator has an electric element for heat and a fan and vents for air circulation. Dehydrators are efficiently designed to dry foods quickly at 140° F (60° C). They are widely available in stores and online. Costs vary widely, depending on the features of each model. The most expensive and efficient ones have stackable trays, horizontal air flow, and thermostats.

Solar Dryers

Solar dryers are highly effective, and yield results on par with electric dehydrators, but without the expense and carbon footprint associated with using electricity. Solar dryers don't require a low-humidity climate, although they do require sunshine and high temperatures. The only downside is the requirement that you assemble or build your own dryer. Storage may not be an issue since they are designed to be used outdoors.

Equipment If you are handy with tools, consider building a solar-powered food dryer. There are plenty of kits available online, or you can build from your own design. A solar dryer has three basic parts: a solar collector (such as an old storm window), a box to hold the food, and a stand. The collector captures the heat of the sun to warm air that will circulate around the food. The box is usually made from plywood and holds food trays, which are made from screening to allow greatest air circulation. The most sophisticated solar designs include adjustable vents and thermostats.

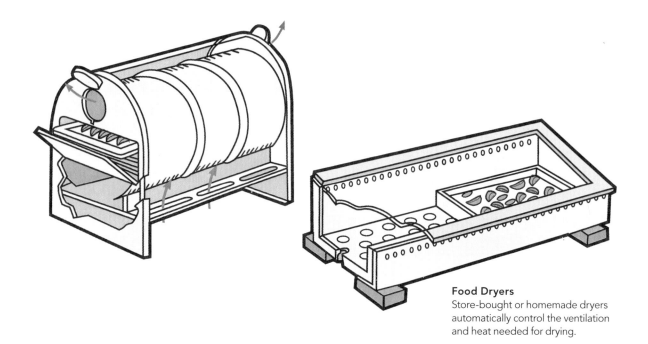

Food Dryers
Store-bought or homemade dryers automatically control the ventilation and heat needed for drying.

Method: Building Your Own Solar Dryer

1 Set a tall, nearly square cardboard box on a table or a chair support. Cover with a cloth screen. This is the drying box.

2 Using some tape, attach the short flap of a long, thin, cardboard box to the drying box, as shown in the diagram. This will be the solar collector. Make sure that the collector faces toward the sun. Line the bottom of the collector box with a black plastic garbage bag. Cover the top of the collector with clear plastic wrap or glass, using tape to hold it all together.

3 If you want to increase the efficiency of your solar food dryer, cover the sides and bottoms of both boxes with fiberglass or Styrofoam insulation.

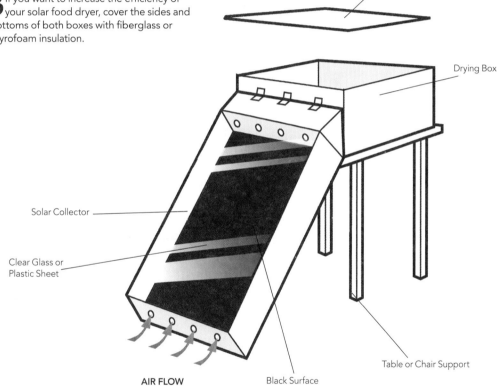

Cloth Screen

Drying Box

Solar Collector

Clear Glass or Plastic Sheet

Table or Chair Support

AIR FLOW

Black Surface

Homemade Solar Dryers To dry food with the sun, you need at least 3–5 consecutive days of sunshine. You cannot stop and start the process.

Pasteurizing Sun-Dried Fruits and Vine-Dried Beans

Pasteurizing is necessary to kill any insects and their eggs that might be on the food. Unless destroyed, the insects will eat the dried food. To pasteurize in the freezer, seal the dried food in freezer-type plastic bags. Place the bags in a freezer set at 0° F (-17° C) or below and leave them at least 48 hours. Alternatively, you can arrange the dried food on trays in a single layer, place the trays in an oven preheated to 160° F (70° C), and leave for 30 minutes. After either of these treatments, the dried fruit is ready to be conditioned and stored.

Making It Easy:
Sun-Dried Tomatoes

Tomatoes are an easy vegetable to dry—and easy to use. Just soak the dried tomatoes in warm water for 30 minutes and they will become soft and pliable, ready to use in soups, sauces, even casseroles and quiches. (Reserve the soaking liquid to add flavor to stocks and sauces.) Once reconstituted, use sun-dried tomatoes within several days or pack them in olive oil and store in the refrigerator for up to 2 weeks. To use oil-packed tomatoes, lift the tomatoes from the oil. Keep the tomatoes left in the jar completely covered with olive oil, which may mean adding more oil as you use some of the tomatoes. Add a sprig of basil and a clove of garlic for extra flavor, if you like. Don't toss out that oil when you're done with the tomatoes. It will pick up flavor from the tomatoes and be delicious in salad dressings or used for sautéing.

ONCE THE FOOD IS DRY

To make the most of your dried food, you must ensure that you store it appropriately, in a dry, dark place.

Storing Dried Foods

Before packaging dried foods for storage, cool them completely in clean, moisture-resistant containers. Glass jars, metal cans, and freezer tubs with tight-fitting lids are good storage containers. Plastic freezer bags are acceptable, but they are not insect- and rodent-proof. Place fruit in a plastic bag before storing it in a metal can.

Dried food needs to be stored in a cool, dry, dark place. Most dried fruits can be stored for one year at 60° F (15° C), or six months at 80° F (30° C). Dried vegetables have about half the shelf-life of fruits. Fruit leathers (see page 61) should keep for up to one month at room temperature. To store any dried product longer, place it in the freezer.

Reconstituting Dried Foods

Dried fruits can be eaten as is or reconstituted. Dried vegetables must be reconstituted. Once reconstituted, dried fruits or vegetables are treated as fresh. Fruit leathers and meat jerky are eaten as is.

To reconstitute dried fruits or vegetables, add water to the fruit or vegetable and soak until the desired volume is restored. For soups and stews, add the dehydrated vegetables without rehydrating them. They will rehydrate as the soup or stew cooks. Also, leafy vegetables and tomatoes do not need soaking. Add enough water to cover, and simmer until tender.

Method: Making Fruit Leathers

Fruit leather is a tasty, chewy way to enjoy dried fruit. Fruit leathers are made by pouring puréed fruit onto a flat surface for drying. When dried, the fruit is pulled from the surface and rolled. It gets the name "leather" because it has the texture of leather.

1 Select ripe fruit or use canned and drained, or frozen and defrosted, fruit. Wash fresh fruit or berries in cool water. Remove peel, seeds, and stem.

2 Cut fruit into chunks. Use 2 cups (300 g) of fruit for each 13- by 15-inch (35- by 40-cm) fruit leather. Purée the fruit until smooth.

3 Add 2 teaspoons (30 ml) (10 ml) of lemon juice or a pinch of ascorbic acid for every 2 cups (750 g) of light-colored fruit to prevent darkening. Sweeten to taste with corn syrup, honey, or sugar.

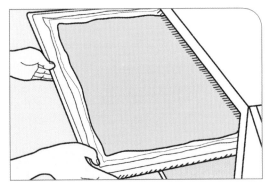

4 Line cookie sheets with plastic wrap. In a dehydrator, use plastic wrap or the specially designed plastic sheets that come with the dehydrator. Pour the purée onto the lined cookie sheets or dehydrator trays. Spread it evenly to a thickness of ⅛ inch (3 mm).

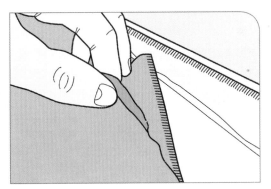

5 Dry at 140° F (60° C) until no indention is left when you touch the center with your finger. This takes 6–8 hours in a dehydrator, up to 18 hours in the oven, and 1–2 days in the sun. While still warm, peel from the plastic wrap. Cool, rewrap in plastic, and store.

PRESERVING VEGETABLES

Before you start preserving, give some thought to how you will use each vegetable. If you are a last-minute sort of cook, you may prefer to have your tomatoes canned and ready to use, rather than frozen or dried. If you do a lot of backpacking, needing lightweight supplies may make drying foods particularly appealing. If you have a root cellar or comparable space, storing vegetables there makes the most sense because it is so fast and easy. Although a vegetable can be preserved in a number of ways, usually one method is more successful than the others for each different crop. Cabbage is best stored in a root cellar, whereas corn keeps its flavor best when frozen.

Timing, temperatures, types, containers, and alternative methods tend to change between vegetable families and from one vegetable to another, so it is useful to have a general guide to preserving the various crops in your harvest. There are always ways to cut corners and save time, so preserving vegetables can be as simple as you make it. Time-intensive pickles and chutneys taste fantastic, but it is just as rewarding to grab some homegrown peas from the freezer for supper.

MAKING THE MOST OF YOUR VEGETABLES

The vegetables in this chapter are arranged into groups that share similarities in terms of which parts of the plant we eat. Many also share similarities in how they are preserved. Most of the vegetables that can be frozen can also be pressure-canned (see page 51 for canning times); unless they are pickled, do not use a boiling-water bath for vegetables other than tomatoes. Most of the vegetables that can be frozen can also be dried; don't forget to blanch before drying, unless otherwise specified (see page 81 for blanching times). All vegetables need to be washed before they are dried, frozen, canned, pickled, or juiced. Do not wash vegetables before storing in a root cellar.

BEANS, SEEDS, PODS, AND LEGUMES

With the exception of dried beans (navy, kidney, butter, great northern, lima, and soybeans, for example) and some legumes (lentils), these vegetables freeze well, which is the preferred way to preserve them.

Dried Beans

Dried beans are full of flavor. Freshly dried beans also take much less time to cook than regular beans.

Beans There are many varieties of bean types—they are a valuable source of protein.

Harvest Leave the bean pods on the vine in the garden until the beans inside rattle and the vines and pods are dry and shriveled.

Best Method: Dry Shell the beans and discard the pods. Do not wash, which would introduce moisture. If the beans are still moist, complete the drying process in the sun, oven, or a dehydrator to avoid possible mold.

Green Beans (snap beans, wax beans, haricot verts, Italian green beans)

High-quality green beans are crisp and tender without scars. Well-shaped pods with small seeds are desirable. Green beans should feel pliable and velvety, not hard or tough.

Harvest Pick young tender beans that snap when broken, with seeds that are small and tender.

Best Method: Freeze Green beans are best preserved frozen. Snip off the tips and sort for size. Cut or break into suitable pieces or leave whole. Blanch, chill, package, and freeze.

Other Methods Alternatively, green beans can be pickled (see Dilly Beans recipe, page 110), pressure-canned, or dried.

Shell Beans

Shell beans are the seeds of legumes that are harvested while still green. Lima beans are a type of shell bean.

Harvest Pick well-filled pods containing young tender beans. Shell the beans and discard the pods.

Best Method: Freeze Blanch and chill. Tray-freeze for 30 minutes, then pack into freezer bags.

Other Methods Shell beans can also be pressure-canned.

Leather Britches Green beans can be threaded on a string with minimal effort and left to dry in the sun or over a woodstove.

Making It Easy:
Leather Britches

In the old days, when folks used to preserve all their garden produce to see them through the winter, they dried green beans and called them leather britches.

Try making your own: Thread a large darning needle with cotton string and string up the beans, sticking the needle through the middle of each bean so both ends of the bean are loose. Dry in a sunny window or over a woodstove until the beans are dry and wrinkled.

To cook, remove from the string, rinse well, and bring to a boil in a large pot of water. Drain well. Now the beans are ready to cook. In the old days, they were stewed with a ham bone, onion, and plenty of salt and pepper, and maybe a hot pepper as well. Cook until tender.

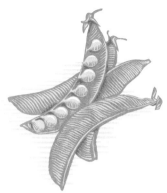

Peas Peas retain their sweet and delicious flavor even after prolonged freezing.

Peas (green or English, sugar snap, snow peas)

Peas are cool-season vegetables that can withstand frost. They are packed with nutrients, making them the ultimate convenience food.

Harvest Pick green and sugar snap peas when the pods are plump and crisp, filled with tender, sweet peas. Overmature peas are starchy. Pick snow peas as soon as the pods reach their full length but before the peas within develop.

Best Method: Freeze Both types need to be blanched, chilled in ice water, and drained well. Tray-freeze for 30 minutes. Transfer to freezer bags and freeze.

Other Methods Peas can also be pressure-canned or dried.

CORN

New supersweet varieties of corn make it possible to delay preserving without a complete loss of flavor and sweetness.

Harvest Harvest early in the morning if the weather is hot, and plan to preserve as soon as possible. It is important to pick corn at its peak of ripeness. If corn is immature, it will be watery when cooked; if it is too mature, it will be starchy. Husk each ear, remove the silks, and trim the ends.

Freezing Corn Remove the kernels, pointing the knife away from you to prevent injury.

Best Method: Freeze on the Cob Bring a large pot of water to a boil and blanch just a few ears at a time. Thoroughly chill the blanched ears in ice water; corn that is frozen while still warm may become mushy or taste strongly of the cob. Drain, dry, and wrap the ears individually in plastic wrap. Then freeze in plastic bags.

Freeze Kernels Stand the cobs upright and slice down to remove the kernels. Blanch, chill, and drain. Tray-freeze for 30 minutes, then pack in freezer bags and freeze.

Other Methods Corn kernels can also be pressure-canned or dried, or made into a high-acid relish and canned in a boiling-water bath.

OKRA

Okra, also called gumbo or ladyfingers, is a warm-season vegetable that grows well throughout the Southeast United States and Texas.

Harvest Harvest when the pods are 2–3 inches (5–7.5 cm) long.

Best Method: Freeze Remove the stem ends, being careful not to cut into the seed pods. Blanch, cool, and drain. Leave whole or slice crosswise. Tray-freeze for 30 minutes. Transfer to bags and freeze.

For fried okra, slice the blanched pods crosswise and dredge in flour or cornmeal. Spread in a single layer on a shallow pan. Freeze just until firm. Package and freeze.

Other Methods Pickle whole okra pods in a sweetened vinegar brine and process in a boiling-water bath. Okra can also be pressure-canned or dried.

CABBAGE FAMILY

The vegetables in this family are not recommended for drying because overly strong flavors develop. White or green cabbages and Chinese cabbages, including bok choy, are good keepers in cold storage; broccoli, brussels sprouts, and cauliflower are best frozen.

Cabbage-family vegetables are often infested with cabbage worms, which are perfectly camouflaged against the green stems. Cabbage worms are the larvae of cabbage white butterflies, and sometimes it can be difficult to recognize them.

The full-grown butterfly is about 2 inches (5 cm) wide and has off-white wings with gray spots. If you see them near your cabbage, it's time to look for the larvae and eggs. The larvae do the damage and are velvety green worms about an inch (2.5 cm) long. If you see the eggs, you may have caught them in time; they are yellow and oval-shaped.

To get rid of these pests, soak in a salt brine (½ cup or 120 g salt to 4 cups or 950 ml water) for 30 minutes before preserving. Cabbage worms, if present, will float to the surface of the water.

Cabbage This is one vegetable that preserves very well in cold storage, but the cold storage room requires good ventilation.

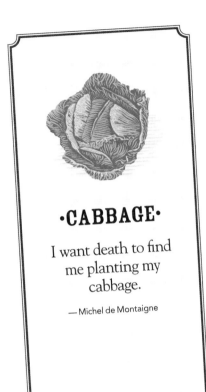

·CABBAGE·

I want death to find
me planting my
cabbage.

— Michel de Montaigne

Broccoli

Broccoli has long been known to decrease the risk of cancer and to generally be good for health, due in part to its high vitamin A and C content.

Harvest Harvest when the head is fully formed and dark green; the buds should be tight. Yellow flowers indicate that the broccoli has been left on the stem too long. Once the main head is harvested, smaller side heads will form and can be handled the same as the main head.

Best Method: Freeze Remove tough leaves and woody ends. Cut through the stalks lengthwise, leaving heads of about 1 inch (2.5 cm) in diameter, or cut into chunks. Blanch, chill, package, and freeze.

Brussels Sprouts

Brussels sprouts are hardy, slow-growing, long-season vegetables. They are a good source of fiber.

Harvest Pick when the stalks produce full-sized, firm, compact heads of vibrant green color, and harvest before they turn yellow and toughen. Sprouts will keep in good shape in the garden and withstand light frosts, becoming purple-tinged but remaining high in quality.

Cold Storage You will get a few extra weeks of harvest by pulling the whole plant up and hanging it upside down in a root cellar. Then harvest sprouts as you need them, starting at the root end.

Best Method: Freeze Trim the sprouts by removing the outer leaves and cutting an X at the stem end to ensure even cooking. Blanch and chill. Drain and spread on a tray in a single layer. Cover with plastic wrap to prevent odors from permeating the freezer. Freeze for 30 minutes, pack into plastic bags, and freeze.

Cabbages

Cabbages include red, green, or white cabbages and Chinese cabbages, including bok choy.

Harvest Leave cabbage in the garden as late in the fall as possible, but harvest before the heads start to split. If the heads threaten to split, give them a twist to break off some of the roots and slow the growth. Repeat every 7–10 days. Cut the head off each stem.

Best Method: Cold Storage Green and white cabbages have the best keeping qualities. Savoy cabbage can withstand the coldest

temperatures, making it the best candidate for keeping in the garden for as long as possible. Red cabbages and bok choy keep less well than green cabbages. Remove stems and loose leaves and wrap in newspaper or burlap. Store in a cold, damp area, preferably where temperatures are just barely above freezing.

Pickle Cabbage may be made into sauerkraut or Korean kimchi or pickled as a relish and canned in a boiling-water bath.

Cauliflower
Cauliflower is fussy to grow, but tastes delicious and freezes very well.

Harvest When the head is tight and uniform, harvest by cutting the head off the stem. If the curds start to separate, the cauliflower has gone by.

Best Method: Freeze Trim the heads. Split into 1-inch (2.5-cm) pieces. Blanch, chill, package, and freeze.

Other Methods Cauliflower will keep for about a month in a root cellar. It can also be pickled and canned in a boiling-water bath.

Kohlrabi
Kohlrabi has appeared only in the past few hundred years. However, it can be grown almost anywhere and in almost any conditions. This German turnip has a mild and sweet taste, similar to cabbage heart or broccoli stem.

Harvest Kohlrabi are ready to harvest when the bulbs are 2–3 inches (5–7.5 cm) in diameter.

Best Method: Cold Storage Trim off the leaves and roots and store in a cold, damp area, preferably where the temperatures are just above freezing.

Freeze Peel the bulbs, cut into cubes, blanch, chill, package, and freeze.

Cabbage Varieties All types of cabbage preserve very well in cold storage, though Chinese varieties will need to be eaten sooner.

Kohlrabi This odd-looking vegetable can be peeled and eaten raw or prepared as you would broccoli.

FRUIT VEGETABLES

This group of vegetables includes chiles, sweet peppers, eggplant, and tomatoes. Tomatoes are the most versatile in terms of potential methods of preserving; eggplant are the least.

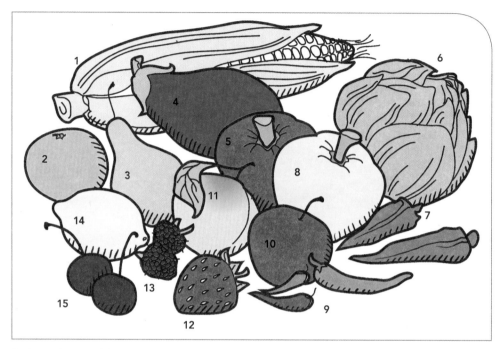

Fruits and Vegetables
1 Corn 2 Orange 3 Pear 4 Eggplant 5 Red Bell Pepper 6 Lettuce 7 Green Chiles 8 Yellow Bell Pepper 9 Chiles 10 Apple 11 Peach 12 Strawberry 13 Blackberries 14 Lemon 15 Cherries

Chiles and Peppers

Chiles are excellent dried, frozen, or pickled. They can be pressure-canned.

Harvest Peppers and chiles are the rare vegetables that can be harvested and enjoyed unripe (green) or left to ripen until fully ripe (usually red). They are sweeter when fully red. If harvested unripe, the plant will continue to set fruit. For drying, harvest peppers and chiles when fully ripe.

Best Method: Freeze Remove stems and seeds. Halve, slice, or dice. Blanching is optional. You can freeze chopped peppers without blanching, if you plan to use them in soups and cooked sauces.

Dry There is no need to blanch before drying. To dry sweet peppers, slice into thin strips and dry. Chiles can be dried whole or sliced. Whole chiles can be strung by running a needle and thread through the thickest part of the stem, then dried outdoors, in a sunny window, or near a woodstove. Store in containers or leave hanging in a dry place.

Eggplant

Eggplants are a cold-sensitive vegetable. They require a long warm season for best yields.

Harvest Harvest any time after they have reached half their mature size by cutting off the plant, leaving a short stem. Younger eggplants are more tender, and harvesting at this stage encourages the plant to set more fruit.

Best Method: Freeze Eggplant is best cooked and frozen in a finished dish, such as ratatouille or eggplant Parmesan.

Dry Slice eggplant ¼ inch (5 mm) thick to dry.

Tomatoes

No vegetable has as many preserving options as tomatoes. Tomatoes can be canned in a boiling-water bath, dried, or frozen.

Harvest Pick tomatoes when they are fully ripe and slightly soft to the touch, but if frost threatens before the vegetables are fully ripe, all is not lost. Green tomatoes can be ripened in cold storage or pickled.

Peeling Is Optional. Whether you are canning or freezing whole or chopped tomatoes, peeling is optional. The peel will separate from the tomatoes in both processes and may be considered unappetizing, but it doesn't really affect the final product. To peel tomatoes, dip a few into boiling water for 1 minute. Remove with a slotted spoon and continue until all the tomatoes have been dipped. The peels will be easy to remove.

Tomato Purées Prepare tomato purées for either canning or freezing. Simmer chopped tomatoes in a pan for 5 minutes or until soft. Push through a sieve or food mill to remove skins and seeds.

Cold Storage for Unripened Tomatoes To ripen green tomatoes, pack unbruised green tomatoes in a single layer in shallow boxes or in trays in a root cellar or cool garage. Cover with a few layers of

Making It Easy:
Freezing Tomatoes

Tray-freeze cherry tomatoes and chopped fresh tomatoes, without blanching. Defrost in a colander. The defrosted tomatoes will be ready to use in cooked dishes where the skins will not pose a problem (chunky sauces and soups).

Tomato Purée Ideal for canning or freezing, tomato purée is the basic ingredient in many delicious dishes.

newspaper. Check daily, and remove the tomatoes as they ripen. Remove any tomatoes that show signs of spoilage. Tomatoes stored this way will ripen in 4–6 weeks.

Storing Ripened Tomatoes Ripened tomatoes should be stored at about 55–65° F (15–20° C) and used within a few days. You should not refrigerate tomatoes, because the cold temperature turns the flesh grainy and ruins the flavor.

Can Boiling-water bath canning is a great option for tomatoes because it stores them in a recipe-ready form. Because the acidity of the tomatoes varies, safe canning requires that the tomatoes be acidified. If you are making a chutney or ketchup, which usually contains vinegar, the acid is part of the recipe. Otherwise, acidify the tomatoes by adding 2 tablespoons (25 ml) bottled lemon juice or ½ teaspoon (2 ml) citric acid to each quart (1-liter) jar. Pack tomatoes cut into wedges or puréed. You can hot-pack or raw-pack (see page 42).

Freeze You can freeze tomatoes without blanching. Remove the stems, cut into halves or quarters, or leave whole. Then pack into freezer bags and freeze. Or freeze purées in freezer containers. Cherry tomatoes freeze very well by tray-freezing without blanching.

When using frozen whole or chopped tomatoes, defrost in a colander over a bowl. Use the liquid that drains away as needed in your recipes (you may not need it).

You can also freeze tomatoes already made into salsas or soups. If you freeze an uncooked sauce, such as salsa, let it thaw in a sieve set over a bowl and add back just enough of the thawed juices to achieve a good consistency.

For cooked sauces, core and quarter the tomatoes. Simmer, covered, in a heavy pot until soft, then remove the lid. Add seasonings as desired. As long as you are freezing the sauce, feel free to add other vegetables, such as garlic, onions, and peppers. For stewed tomatoes, simmer for 15–30 minutes. To make a sauce, continue to simmer until the tomatoes are cooked down to a pleasing consistency, for 2–6 hours, depending on the size of your batch.

Dry Dry tomatoes outdoors, in an oven, or in an electric dehydrator. The slower the drying process, the more likely the tomatoes will blacken due to oxidation; they are still fine to eat, however.

Kale and Other Greens
Greens are a staple of Southern cooking in the United States.

GREENS

Greens thrive in a nitrogen-rich soil and are very good sources of vitamins A, C, and K, as well as folate, iron, and calcium. These plants also provide fiber and have been linked to preventing certain types of cancer. Proper storage is needed to maintain that high nutritional value, and greens store easily through several methods.

Chard, Collards, Endive, Escarole, Kale

Kale is notable for withstanding frost and even a blanket of snow, if the roots are well protected by mulch. Collards will keep well in a garden until a killing frost. Endive, escarole, and chard will withstand light frosts.

Harvest Harvest greens at any stage, from baby leaves to full maturity.

Cold Storage Harvest by cutting the stems at the soil level and store in perforated plastic bags in a cold, damp root cellar. Dig up endive, escarole, and chard, roots and all, and replant in boxes of soil or sand in the root cellar.

Freeze Of all the tender greens, only spinach and chard can be frozen. To freeze any green, remove tough stems, then blanch, chill, drain, pack, and freeze.

Other Methods Greens can be dried. They can also be pressure-canned, although many people today find pressure-canned greens unpalatable and overcooked.

ONION FAMILY

Onions, shallots, and garlic are ready for harvest when most of the tops fall over, turn brown, and shrivel at the neck.

Garlic, Onions, and Shallots

Members of the onion family are biennial bulbs, requiring two growing seasons to produce seeds. They can be easily cultivated in temperate climates across the United States.

Best Method: Cold Storage Before storing, cure the bulbs by arranging them in a single layer, off the moist ground and out of direct sun, and leaving them for about 2 weeks. Then remove the tops and place the bulbs in bins or storage bags or

Making It Easy:
Mixed Vegetables for Soup

Freezer bags filled with a mixture of vegetables make the basis of a satisfying vegetable soup. Just add a can of tomatoes, broth (chicken, beef, or vegetable), and seasoning, and you have a delicious soup.

Dice all the vegetables to a uniform size. Blanch a few cups at a time in boiling water for 2–3 minutes. Drain, chill, and drain again. Then pack, label, and freeze.

Onions These vegetables do very well in cold storage and can last until spring. Pickling the smaller varieties is also a popular choice.

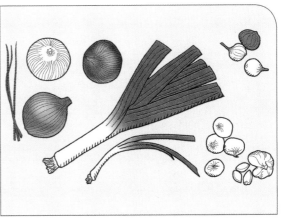

braid their tops together. Onions, shallots, and garlic need dry storage, which an unused room or unheated attic may provide; do not store in a root cellar, which is too damp.

Freeze Garlic, onions, and shallots can be frozen. Chopped onions and shallots can be tray-frozen without blanching and used directly in cooked dishes. Blanching improves quality and extends storage life.

Dry They can also be dried without blanching.

Pickle Garlic and pearl onions are sometimes pickled in a vinegar brine and canned in a boiling-water bath.

Garlic Garlic adds essential flavor to the cooking of the Mediterranean and Asia.

Leeks
Leeks can be kept in the garden under a thick blanket of mulch.

Harvest To harvest, loosen the soil with a garden fork and pull the plants from the ground.

Best Method: Cold Storage Dig up the entire plant and replant in a box of soil or sand in the root cellar.

Freeze Trim off the outer leaves, tops, and root ends. Slice and tray-freeze. Blanching first is not necessary, but the leeks will keep longer if you do.

ROOT VEGETABLES AND TUBERS
Beets, carrots, celery root, Jerusalem artichokes, parsnips, potatoes, rutabagas, salsify, sweet potatoes, and turnips keep best in a root cellar at 32–40° F (0–4° C) and 90 percent humidity. Before storing in the root cellar, trim off the tops, but don't trim the roots. Lightly brush off loose dirt, but don't wash. Handle the vegetables gently. These vegetables can also be pressure-canned.

Beets
There are many varieties of beets, including some that are golden and striped red and white.

Beets For even more color, combine red and golden beets on the same plate.

Harvest Harvest at any size; small beets tend to be more flavorful. Harvest by grasping at the base of the greens and gently pulling up.

Best Method: Cold Storage Layer beets in moist sand or sawdust and store in a root cellar.

Other Methods Fully cooked beets can be sliced or diced and frozen, or pickled and processed in a boiling-water bath, or dried. They can also be pressure-canned.

Root Vegetables and Tubers
Although root vegetables can be stored in the garden and allowed to freeze, tubers (potatoes and sweet potatoes) must not be allowed to freeze.

Carrots

When planting carrots, make sure to select varieties that are bred for cold storage, if that is how you plan to preserve them.

Harvest Harvest at any size by pulling gently at the base of the tops.

Best Method: Cold Storage For enjoying raw and in salads, carrots are best stored in a root cellar, layered in moist sand or sawdust.

Other Methods Carrots can also be sliced or diced, blanched, chilled, and frozen or dried. Carrots are sometimes pickled in jars of mixed vegetable pickles. They can also be pressure-canned.

Celery Root (Celeriac)

Celery root (celeriac) is not the root of a celery plant, but a different vegetable in its own right, though from the same family.

Harvest Loosen the soil around each plant and pull gently to harvest.

Cold Storage Layer in moist sand or sawdust and store in a root cellar.

Jerusalem Artichokes

Jerusalem artichokes can be preserved by storing them in the ground or in a root cellar, cooking and freezing them, or using them in prepared dishes and then freezing. They can also be pickled.

Carrots Carrots store well in a root cellar and are good candidates for freezing.

Harvest Leave in the ground and continue to harvest as long as the soil can be dug. They have best flavor after a few hard frosts. Dig up with a garden fork, and gather only as many roots as needed. The plants are perennials.

Cold Storage In the root cellar, Jerusalem artichokes will keep for 1–2 months, layered in moist sand or sawdust.

Parsnips and Salsify

Parsnips are a biennial root vegetable and a member of the parsley family. Their roots develop a sweetness after being exposed to cold for a few weeks. Salsify is also called oyster plant, because it has a taste strikingly similar to oysters when cooked.

Harvest Parsnips and salsify can be left in the ground under a thick mulch and harvested in the spring; freezing sweetens these vegetables. Loosen the soil with a garden fork and carefully pull up the roots.

Best Method: Cold Storage They are good keepers in a root cellar, layered in moist sand or sawdust.

Other Methods They can also be sliced or diced, blanched, chilled, and frozen.

Potatoes

Grow both russet or baking types as well as thin-skinned waxy or all-purpose potatoes.

Harvest When the green tops on potatoes die off, the underground tubers can be harvested. Carefully loosen the soil and feel around for the tubers. Brush off the loose dirt and arrange them in a single layer off the moist ground to cure in the shade for 2 weeks. (Do not cure in the sun because this will turn the tubers green and make them harmful to eat.)

Potatoes An advantage of growing your own potatoes is being able to choose from among the hundreds of varieties available—including blue-, yellow-, and pink-fleshed varieties.

Best Method: Cold Storage Once cured, move potatoes to a cold, damp root cellar. Store them in a bin or a pile covered with straw or burlap.

Freeze For French fries, russets or baking potatoes freeze best. Peel and remove any eyes, bruises, or green flesh. Cut into ¼–½-inch (0.5–1-cm) matchsticks. Blanch, drain well, and tray-freeze for 30 minutes. Then package and freeze. For hash browns, choose waxy potatoes, and cook unpeeled potatoes until almost done. Then peel, grate, and form into patties. Tray-freeze for 1 hour, then package and freeze.

Dry For chips, slice thinly and dry.

Rutabagas and Turnips

Turnips and rutabagas are closely related but are different vegetables botanically. Turnips are smaller and less sweet than rutabagas.

Harvest Harvest at any size by pulling gently at the base of the tops.

Best Method: Cold Storage Store in a root cellar, layered in moist sand or sawdust.

Other Methods Small, young roots can be frozen or pressure-canned; older roots will be too strongly flavored.

Sweet Potatoes

Sweet potatoes most commonly have bright orange or pale yellow flesh. The sweet, bright orange varieties grow especially well in warmer climates; drier, pale yellow varieties are more common in cooler regions. There are also red and even purple varieties.

Harvest Harvest sweet potatoes whenever they are of usable size. Be sure to harvest before the first frost. Cut back the vines and lift the roots from the ground with a garden fork, taking care to avoid harming the tubers.

Storage Cure freshly harvested sweet potatoes in a warm, damp place—aim for 80–85° F (25–30° C) and 90 percent humidity—to toughen their skins and encourage healing of small scratches. After 10–14 days of curing, wrap the potatoes individually in newspaper, sort them for size, pack them in cartons, and keep them in a cool room.

·POTATOES·

My idea of heaven is a great big baked potato and someone to share it with.

— Oprah Winfrey

Celery Harvesting celery early can result in an even longer picking season.

SHOOTS AND STEMS

This vegetable group includes asparagus, celery, and globe artichokes.

Asparagus

Asparagus has medicinal value, because it has diuretic properties. It is also low in calories, contains no fat or cholesterol and is low in sodium.

Harvest Harvest bright-colored stalks that snap when broken and have tight heads. Cut or snap off the stems at the soil level.

Best Method: Freeze Discard woody and blemished stalks. Break off fibrous ends. Leave whole or cut in 1–2-inch (2.5–5-cm) lengths. Blanch, chill, and freeze.

Other Methods Dry or pressure-can.

Celery

Celery is great for adding texture and flavor to soups and sauces. It is best in the summer months, but it can be easily stored for use in winter.

Harvest Harvest the outer stems of the plant as needed as soon as they reach a useful size. Harvest whole plants by cutting them just at the soil line.

Best Method: Cold Storage Celery can be stored in a trench in the garden, well covered with mulch, provided the trench is well drained. Otherwise, dig up whole plants with the roots, and plant in moist sand or soil in a root cellar.

Other Methods Young, tender stalks can be frozen or dried to use in cooked dishes. Cut into 1-inch (2.5-cm) pieces and blanch. Chill, drain, and tray-freeze for 30 minutes or dry.

Globe Artichokes

Globe artichokes are a pretty vegetable that originated in the Mediterranean. They do not grow in the wild.

Harvest Harvest artichokes when the bud is firm, tight, and an even green color. The first bud to harvest is the terminal bud at the top. Within days the side buds will be ready. Cut the buds off at the base.

Best Method: Freeze To prepare for freezing, remove the outer leaves. Wash and trim the stalks. Remove the "chokes," or fuzzy portion. Blanch a few at a time, chill, and freeze.

Other Methods Artichokes can also be prepared as with freezing and then dried.

VINE VEGETABLES

Cucumbers, pumpkins, summer squash, and winter squash are all vine vegetables. Harvest by cutting off the vine, leaving a small stub of stem.

Cucumbers

Cucumbers are vines that fruit in the warmer months of the year. They are part of the squash family.

Best Method: Pickle Cucumbers are best pickled (see page 98). They can then be processed in a boiling-water bath. There are recipes for freezer pickles as well (see page 104). Cucumber pickles will have the best texture if the cucumbers are harvested when small, before the seeds have fully developed. This will also encourage the plant to continue to produce.

Summer Squash

Summer squash is a category of vegetables that includes zucchini, crookneck, straightneck, scallop, pattypan, and cocozelle. They are best harvested young, which will encourage the plant to continue to produce.

Best Method: Freeze Sliced squash can be blanched, chilled, drained, packaged, and frozen. For use in baked goods, grate squash and steam-blanch for 1–2 minutes, pack hot into containers, and cool the containers by immersing them in cold water. Seal and freeze. Defrost in a colander to discard excess liquid.

Other Methods Summer squash can be pressure-canned or dried.

Cucumbers This vegetable has been carried around the world, and each nation has had an effect on its evolution. Asian cucumbers have the deepest flavor and best crunch.

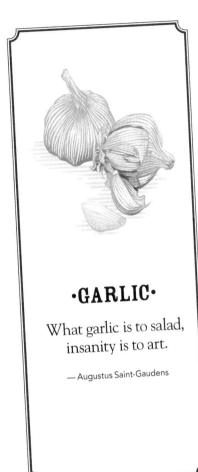

·GARLIC·

What garlic is to salad,
insanity is to art.

— Augustus Saint-Gaudens

Winter Squash and Pumpkins

When mature and removed from the vine, these fruits are still alive. Proper curing and storage slows the rate of respiration and prolongs the storage life of the fruit.

Harvest Harvest when the stems have begun to shrivel and dry and the skin is hard. Harvest by cutting off the vine, leaving a few inches of stem attached to help prevent pathogens from entering the flesh. Let sit outside for a few days to harden the shells. They are considered cured when the shells are hard enough to resist splitting if you try to cut by pushing in a thumbnail.

Best Method: Cold Storage Store in a cool, dry room, such as an attic. Do not store in a root cellar, which is too damp.

Freeze Pumpkin and winter squash can be frozen. Fully cook by baking or steaming, then purée the flesh and freeze.

Pumpkin Pumpkins that are still small and green can be treated like zucchini or squash. They are good mashed or used in a soup.

BLANCHING TIMES FOR VEGETABLES

Before freezing or drying, most vegetables should be blanched in steam or boiling water. When blanching in water, use 1 gallon (3.75 L) of water per pound (450 g) of vegetables, and begin counting the time when the water returns to a boil. When blanching in steam, work in batches of 1 pound (450 g) or less and begin counting the time as soon as the vegetables are placed in the water. When the vegetables are blanched, drain and then plunge into ice water to stop the cooking. Drain thoroughly.

VEGETABLE	BLANCHING TIME (minutes)
Artichoke, Globe (hearts)	7
Asparagus	2–4
Beans: Snap, Green, or Wax	3
Beans: Lima, Butter	2–4
Broccoli (florets 1½ inches/4 cm across)	3
Brussels Sprouts	3–5
Cabbage or Bok Choy (shredded)	1½
Carrots (diced or sliced)	2–5
Cauliflower (florets, 1 inch/2.5 cm across)	3
Corn	
Corn-on-the-cob	7–11
Whole kernel	4
Greens	
Collards	3
All other	2
Kohlrabi (cubes)	1
Okra	3–4
Parsnip (cubes)	2
Peas, edible pod	1½–3
Peas, Green	1½
Peppers, Sweet (strips or rings)	2
Rutabagas (cubes)	3
Shell beans	5
Squash, Chayote	2
Squash, Summer	3
Turnips (cubes)	2

PRESERVING FRUIT

M ost of the techniques that apply to preserving vegetables also apply to preserving fruits, including cold storage, freezing, and drying. Boiling-water bath canning can replace pressure-canning, which is not necessary for fruit. For both freezing and canning, fruit is often packed in sugar or sugar syrup to preserve flavor and color. Some fruits need pretreating to prevent darkening. Of course, almost all fruits can be preserved by making them into jams and jellies of one kind or another (see Jams, Jellies, and Butters, pages 116–133).

In this chapter, the fruits are arranged by family, since related fruits are treated similarly. Fruit should be washed and well dried before it is preserved, unless it is going into cold storage. There are good and bad points to each method of preservation. Freezing fruit, for example, breaks down cell walls, which softens the flesh. This means that frozen fruits are best used in baked desserts and sauces (and freezing your cherry pie filling in advance makes a delicious dessert much quicker to prepare). How you preserve your fruit depends on how you intend to use it. Apricots may be best canned (see page 92 for canning times and page 93 for sugar syrup formulations), but if you want to snack on them, drying is preferable. Try each method for preserving your fruits, and you might just find that each is your favorite in a different way!

THE FRUITS OF YOUR LABOR

Preserving your harvested fruit is deeply rewarding. Preserved fruit snacks, pie fillings, jams, jellies, butters, and smoothies are always a big hit with the family. See page 92 for canning times and page 93 for sugar syrup formulas.

APPLES AND PEARS

Apples and pears are both firm fruits that store well and dry beautifully. They can also be canned or frozen in various forms.

Apples

In addition to the storage options below, apples can be pickled, made into jelly, or made into apple butter.

> ### PREVENTING FRUIT FROM DARKENING
>
> After they are cut or peeled, many fruits (including apples, pears, and peaches) will discolor. To prevent this, drop the fruit in a solution made from 4 quarts (3.75 L) water and 1 teaspoon (5 ml) crushed vitamin C tablets (3,000 mg ascorbic acid).

Best Method: Cold Storage Apples will keep from 1 to 7 months in cold storage, depending on the variety, how quickly the apples were stored after harvest, and how cold you can keep the ambient temperatures. Sort apples and store only unblemished and unbruised apples. Wrap individually in newspaper and layer in cardboard boxes or bins. Do not store near potatoes, which release a gas that hastens spoilage in apples. Remove spoiled apples quickly.

Canning Apples can be canned as applesauce, compote, or slices.

To Make Applesauce Quarter the apples, put them in a pot with just enough water to prevent scorching, cover, and simmer until very soft. Run the apples through a food mill to discard seeds and peels; the peels will give the sauce a rosy hue. Alternatively, for white applesauce, peel before cooking. Sweeten to taste. Pack hot into jars, leaving ½ inch (1 cm) headspace, and process in a boiling-water bath.

To Can as Slices Peel, core, and slice the apples. Pretreat in an ascorbic acid solution to prevent browning. Hot-pack in a light, medium, or heavy syrup, leaving ½ inch (1 cm) headspace, and process in a boiling-water bath.

Dry Pretreat with ascorbic acid to prevent browning. Peel, slice into rings, and dry. Or make fruit leather (see page 61). Finding uses for your dried or dehydrated apple slices is easy, and they can be a chewy and sweet treat during the year when apples are off-season. If you choose to leave your apples dried, mix them with your favorite nuts and oats for a delicious granola. Or you can refresh your dried apples by soaking them in equal parts water to apples for at least half an hour per cup (250 ml) of apples. When the apples are rehydrated, sprinkle them with cinnamon and use them in warm oatmeal or bake them in a tasty apple pie or tart.

Freeze You can freeze applesauce instead of canning it. Make the applesauce as above, pack into freezer containers, and freeze. Or freeze slices in a medium sugar syrup (see page 93) to which you have added ½ teaspoon (2 ml) crushed vitamin C tablets (1,500 mg ascorbic acid). To use, defrost overnight in the refrigerator.

Pears

Pears need to be picked before they are fully ripe for best results. Before canning or freezing, allow pears to ripen at room temperature for 1 day. The gritty texture of the flesh makes it unsuitable for sauces.

Cold Storage Sort and store only unblemished and unbruised pears. Wrap individually in newspaper, layer in cardboard boxes or bins, and store for 1–3 weeks.

Best Method: Can Pears can be canned as slices in a raw-pack or hot-pack. Spiced pears are delicious. To can as slices, peel, core, and slice. Pretreat in an ascorbic acid solution (see page 84) to prevent browning. Hot-pack in a light or medium syrup

Making It Easy:
Apples from the Root Cellar

Toward the end of the winter, apples in the root cellar aren't as crisp and juicy as they were when they first went in. It isn't a problem for desserts made with apples: think pies, crisps, baked apples, and applesauce. All can be made with apples that are older. Just be sure to remove all bruises and damaged spots. And discard any apples that show any signs of mold.

or in apple juice or white grape juice, leaving ½ inch (1 cm) headspace, and process in a boiling-water bath.

Dry Pretreat with ascorbic acid to prevent browning. Peel and slice. Dry slices, or make into fruit leather.

Freeze Freeze slices in a sugar syrup (see page 93) to which you have added ½ teaspoon (2 ml) crushed vitamin C tablets (1,500 mg ascorbic acid).

BERRIES

Berries are a big group, but they can be divided into two subgroups: firm berries and soft berries. Cranberries are considered separately because of their different properties.

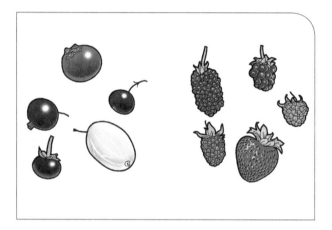

Firm Berries

This group includes blueberries, elderberries, currants, gooseberries, and huckleberries.

Best Method: Freeze Freezing is an excellent option for berries. Tray-freeze berries for making into jams and jellies at a later date. Or pack in a medium syrup or in sugar, using ½ cup (100 g) sugar for every 4 cups (600 g) fruit.

Can Blanch berries in boiling water for 30 seconds. Hot-pack in boiling syrup or juice, leaving ½ inch (1 cm) headspace, and process in a boiling-water bath.

Dry Blanch in boiling water for 15–30 seconds. Drain well, then dry. Not recommended for fruit leathers.

Raspberries Growing raspberries at home allows you to transport them from the garden to the table without fear of crushing them.

Soft Berries

This group includes blackberries, dewberries, loganberries, raspberries, and strawberries.

Best Method: Freeze Freezing is an excellent option for these berries. Tray-freeze berries for making into jams and jellies at a later date. Or pack in a medium syrup or in sugar, using ¾ cup (150 g) sugar for every 4 cups (600 g) fruit.

Can Raw-pack in a light or medium syrup, leaving ½ inch (1 cm) headspace, and process in a boiling-water bath.

Dry Seedy berries are not recommended for drying, but their purées make excellent fruit leathers.

CRANBERRIES

Cranberries are a native fruit of North America. They grow on trailing vines and thrive on the unique soils and water of cranberry bogs.

Best Method: Freeze Cranberries can be packed into bags and frozen dry. The freezing will cause very little change in the fruit.

Can Make into cranberry sauce by combining 4 cups (600 g) berries, 1 cup (250 ml) water, and 2 cups (375 g) sugar. Boil until thick, about 5 minutes. Hot-pack into jars, leaving ½ inch (1 cm) headspace, and process in a boiling-water bath.

Dry Cranberries are easy to dry. Turn the oven on for 10 minutes at 350° F (175° C). Then place the cranberries on a cookie sheet in the oven, turn off the oven, and let them sit overnight. Keep in mind that dried cranberries can be used in place of raisins in recipes.

Strawberries This international favorite has many delicious uses in preserves, smoothies, and desserts.

Making It Easy:
Berry Sherbet

A quick and simple dessert that you can prepare ahead of time, berry sherbet is also very low in fat and can be made sugar-free. All you need is:

- 1 cup (240 ml) skim milk
- 1 cup (240 ml) freshly sliced strawberries, blueberries, and raspberries
- ¼ cup (60 g) sugar or sugar substitute

Pour the milk into divided ice cube trays and freeze until solid, about 2–3 hours. Just before serving, let the frozen milk cubes stand at room temperature for 5 minutes. Place in a food processor, and pulse until milk cubes are broken up. Purée until smooth. Add the berries and sugar (or substitute) in batches, and continue pulsing until smooth. Spoon into dessert dishes to serve immediately, or place in a freezer container and refreeze to desired firmness.

CITRUS FRUITS

This group includes grapefruit, kumquats, oranges, tangelos, tangerines, and mandarins. Lemons and limes are used mainly for flavoring. Select firm fruits that are heavy for their size. Peel and discard any white membrane and seeds. Citrus fruits are not recommended for drying because they are too juicy.

Best Method: Cold Storage The best option for citrus fruit is to store it in an open plastic bag or bin in a root cellar, where it will keep for 4–6 weeks.

Freeze Pack in heavy syrup and freeze.

MELONS

Popular melons include cantaloupes (muskmelon), casabas, crenshaws, honeydews, persians, and watermelon. Although they are best enjoyed fresh, they can be peeled, seeded, and cut into cubes. Then pack in a light syrup and freeze.

Best Method: Refrigerate Cut the melon in half, remove any seeds, and cut out the fruit from the rind. You can use a melon baller to create decorative servings, or just slice into cubes. Keep melon in the refrigerator for a few days for a vitamin-rich sweet and tasty snack.

Freeze Mix 9 cups (2 L) fruit juice with 2¼ cups (450 g) sugar to form a syrup, and place fresh, ripe melon into freezer containers with the syrup. Melon will keep in the freezer for up to 12 months.

Citrus Fruit Cold storage is best for citrus produce, but juicing and freezing is another tasty option.

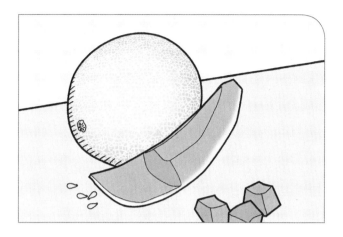

Can Melons are easy to can for delicious, sweet preserves. Combine 2 pounds (900 g) firm, ripe melon, peeled and cut into 1-inch (2.5-cm) slices, with 4 cups (750 g) sugar, and let stand overnight. Add the juice of 1 lemon, and cook in a large pot until clear. Pour into hot, sterilized jars. Adjust lids at once, and process in a boiling-water bath for 5 minutes (see page 46). Makes about 1 quart (1 L).

GRAPES AND CURRANTS

When preparing for freezing, drying, or canning, choose fully ripe, firm, sweet table grapes. Remove stems from grapes and currants. Leave seedless grapes whole; seeded grapes need to be cut in half and seeds removed.

Best Method: Dry Grapes with seeds should be cut in half, then dried. Whole seedless grapes should be cut in half or blanched for 30 seconds, then dried. Currants can be dried whole.

·LEMONS·

When you have
a lemon, make
lemonade.

—Dale Carnegie

RIPENING
GREEN FRUITS

Ripen green fruits by placing them in a perforated plastic bag—the holes allow air movement, and the bag helps retain the odorless gases that promote ripening. Some fruits release more gas as they ripen; combining green fruit with a ripe apple or banana will speed up the process. Place green fruits in a paper bag with a ripe apple or banana and leave for a day or so, and you should find that the green fruit has ripened. Don't leave them too long, though, or they may take on some of the banana's flavor.

Freeze Pack currants and grapes in a medium syrup (see page 93), then freeze.

Can Choose unripe, green, seedless grapes. Blanch in boiling water for 30 seconds. Use a medium syrup for hot-packing or raw-packing, leaving ½ inch (1 cm) headspace, and process in a boiling-water bath.

RHUBARB

Choose firm, tender, well-colored stalks. Do not pick after midsummer. The leaves of rhubarb plants are poisonous and need to be trimmed away. Cut the stem into short lengths.

Rhubarb A traditional dessert staple, rhubarb grows very well in a kitchen garden.

Best Method: Freeze The easiest way to preserve rhubarb is to pack it raw into freezer containers and freeze. It can also be packed in a medium syrup and frozen.

Can Cut into 1-inch (2.5-cm) pieces and combine in a saucepan with ½ cup (100 g) sugar for every 4 cups (600 g) fruit. Let stand until juice appears. Heat to boiling. Hot-pack into jars, leaving ½ inch (1 cm) headspace, and process in a boiling-water bath.

STONE FRUITS

This group includes apricots, cherries, nectarines, peaches, and plums.

Apricots, Nectarines, and Peaches

Choose well-ripened fruits of good color. Freestone varieties are easiest to pit and slice. Blanch in boiling water for 30 seconds to remove skins. Dip in an ascorbic acid solution (see page 84) before processing by any method to prevent darkening.

Best Method: Can Can in medium syrup, using the raw-pack or hot-pack method, and leaving ½ inch (1 cm) headspace. Process in a boiling-water bath.

Dry Dry completely, or dry as a fruit leather.

Freeze Pack in a medium syrup, or dry-pack in ⅔ cup (125 g) sugar for every 4 cups (600 g) of fruit.

Apricots Often bought dried at the grocery store, apricots also make excellent preserves and canned snacks.

Cherries

Stem cherries and pit, using a cherry pitter or sharp paring knife.

Best Method: Freeze Dry-pack tart cherries in sugar, using ¾ cup (150 g) sugar per 4 cups (600 g) fruit. Pack sweet cherries in a medium syrup.

Can Pit or prick skins with a pin to prevent splitting. If pitted, dip in an ascorbic acid solution (see page 84). Pack in a light syrup using a hot-pack or raw-pack, leaving ½ inch (1 cm) headspace. Process in a boiling-water bath.

Dry Cut and pit before drying. Cherries may be made into a fruit leather.

Cherries Sweet cherries are best for eating on their own. Sour cherries make a great pie.

Plums

Select firm, ripe fruit that is soft enough to yield to slight pressure. Leave whole, pricking the skins before canning, or cut in halves or quarters and pit. Freestone varieties are easiest to pit.

Best Method: Dry Dried plums are known as prunes. Leave whole. If sun-drying, blanch in boiling water for 30 seconds. If oven- or dehydrator-drying, simply rinse in tap water.

Freeze Freeze in medium syrup, adding ½ teaspoon (2 ml) ascorbic acid to each quart (L) of syrup.

Can Hot-pack or raw-pack in a light or medium syrup or water, leaving ½ inch (1 cm) headspace, and process in a boiling-water bath.

·BERRIES·

What will come from the briar but the berry?

— Irish proverb

Plums These come in many colors and are juicy and sweet. They are perfect when eaten raw, but also wonderful in many baked dishes and preserves.

BOILING-WATER BATH TIMES FOR CANNING FRUIT

FRUIT	PINT (500-ML) JARS (minutes)	QUART (L) JARS (minutes)
Apples		
sliced, hot-pack	25	25
applesauce, hot-pack	20	25
juice	5	5
Apricots, raw-pack	30	35
Berries		
hot-pack	20	20
raw-pack	20	25
Cherries		
hot-pack	20	25
raw-pack	30	30
Cranberry Sauce	15	15
Grapes		
hot-pack	10	10
raw-pack	15	20
juice	5	5
Nectarines, raw-pack	30	35
Peaches		
hot-pack	25	30
raw-pack	30	35
Pears, hot-pack	25	30
Plums, raw- or hot-pack	25	30
Rhubarb, hot-pack	20	20

Apples Apples are famous for their keeping abilities. With cold storage, the fruit remains delicious and edible for many months.

STORING CANNED FRUIT

Fruit that has been canned using the hot-pack method of a sugar syrup, especially canned peaches, pears, and apples, may show a blue, red, or pink color change after processing. This is sometimes the result of natural chemical changes that occur as fruits are heated and does not affect the results. After canning the fruit in syrup, make sure the jar is not exposed to extreme temperatures. To avoid freezing in extremely cold storage environments, wrap the canned jars with newspaper and place them in heavy cardboard boxes. Cover the boxes with a heavy cloth or a blanket, if necessary. Likewise, avoid storing near furnaces or plumbing to avoid overheating.

Sugar Syrups for Canning and Freezing

To make the syrups, heat the water and sugar together. Bring to a boil and pour over raw fruit in jars for raw-packs. For hot-packs, bring water and sugar to a boil, add fruit, reheat to boiling, and fill jars immediately. Cool and pour over fruit in freezing containers for freezing.

To Make a 7-Quart (7-L) Batch of Sugar Syrup

To make a sugar syrup, combine the water and sugar in a small saucepan and bring to a boil, stirring until the sugar dissolves.

SYRUP TYPE	WATER	SUGAR
Very light	10½ cups (2.5 L)	1¼ cups (300 g)
Light	9 cups (2.1 L)	2½ cups (600 g)
Medium	8¼ cups (1.95 L)	3¾ cups (900 g)
Heavy	7¾ cups (1.8 L)	5¼ cups (1 kg)

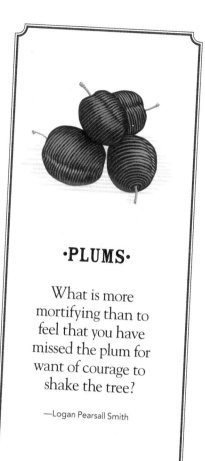

·PLUMS·

What is more mortifying than to feel that you have missed the plum for want of courage to shake the tree?

—Logan Pearsall Smith

Grapes The combination of crunchy texture and dry, sweet, tart flavor has made grapes an ever popular between-meal snack as well as a refreshing addition to both fruit and vegetable salads.

PICKLING

There are two different methods for making pickles: fresh-pack in a vinegar brine and fermented in a salt brine. Chutneys and relishes are a type of fresh-pack pickle; in this case, the vinegar is cooked with the vegetables. For long-term storage, pickles are refrigerated or canned in a boiling-water bath, or you may wish to try some of the newer recipes that have been created for fresh-pack pickles, which are stored in the freezer.

The acidity of pickles keeps them from spoiling, and higher or lower levels of sugar determine the taste. Be sure not to reduce the amount of vinegar called for in a pickling recipe; without enough vinegar, the food could spoil. You can pickle whole or large slices of vegetables or make your favorite condiments.

WHY PICKLE?

Sweet and tasty relishes as well as salsas, sauerkrauts, and even ketchup are perfect projects to practice pickling. The end result makes a great gift, and you can prepare recipes for specific holidays to share with your friends and family.

PREPARING TO PICKLE

Pickling is an easy way of preserving produce for future use. However, there are a few practical things you need to know about how this process works and about which ingredients are the most effective ones to use. Once you have tried a few recipes, experiment with your own ideas to make a signature pickle or condiment for different occasions.

Making It Easy:
Spiced Vinegar

This vinegar recipe adds great flavor to pickles. Use it instead of unflavored white vinegar.

- 2 tablespoons (19 g) mustard seeds
- 2 tablespoons (17 g) black peppercorns
- 2 tablespoons (17 g) allspice berries
- 1 tablespoon (6 g) whole cloves
- fresh ginger
- 10 small dried chiles

Mix the ingredients together and tie in a small square of clean cheesecloth. Add to a saucepan containing 2¼ cups (300 ml) malt vinegar. Bring to a boil and simmer for 10–15 minutes, depending on how strong you want the spice flavor to be. Allow to cool, then discard the spice bag. Bottle and store until required for pickling.

Ingredients

Be sure to use produce that is in prime condition and not wilted, limp, or bruised.

Vegetables Slightly immature, small vegetables will have small seeds and crisp flesh; these make the best pickles, whether you are making bread-and-butters, dilly beans, or pickled zucchini. Avoid overgrown vegetables, which have large seeds and pulpy centers, resulting in mushy pickles. If you are harvesting from your own garden, do not pick in the heat of the day. Store the vegetables in the refrigerator or on ice in insulated coolers.

A pickling cucumber makes a crispier pickle than a salad cucumber. Salad cucumbers can be used as long as they are not waxed (most supermarket cucumbers are waxed). To get started, remove the blossom, which releases enzymes that will soften the pickle, and cut about ¹⁄₁₆ inch (about 2 mm) off the blossom end. Wash all vegetables thoroughly in cool running water. Scrub with a soft vegetable brush to remove any dirt.

Vinegar A key ingredient in making fresh-pack pickles is vinegar. As long as the vinegar has a 40- to 60-grain strength (or 4–6 percent acetic acid), it can be used safely to make pickles. This includes most store-bought vinegars, as well as most homemade herb vinegars made from commercial vinegars.

White distilled vinegar is commonly used because it doesn't compete with the distinctive flavors of the herbs and spices used to make pickles and also because it is very inexpensive. Cider vinegar imparts a rich, fruity flavor that is sometimes desirable, particularly with sweet pickles.

Salt The "pickling salt" used in many recipes is simply table salt without the additives, which can make a pickling liquid cloudy. It is sold in supermarkets. Although you can cut back on the amount of salt you use in fresh-pack pickles, do not alter a recipe for fermented pickles; with these pickles, the salt is the preservative.

Sweeteners Sweeteners will balance the harsh flavor of vinegar. White sugar is preferred because it doesn't darken the pickle (as brown sugar does) or make the brine cloudy (as honey does).

Water Hard water can cause soft pickles. If you live in an area with hard water, use bottled water in your pickles.

Herbs and Spices Use only whole herbs and spices to avoid making the brine cloudy. Dill is a commonly used herb. Sprigs of immature dill can be used interchangeably with mature dill heads.

Equipment

The same equipment used for canning fruit is required for making pickles. Do not use cookware made from brass, copper, galvanized steel, iron, or aluminum, which will react with the acids and salt and produce off flavors. For salt-cured pickles, a crock or large gallon-sized (3.75-L) glass jar is needed. There are pickling crocks available that have cleverly designed tops to exclude air; these are more likely to yield successful pickles than old-fashioned stoneware crocks. A household scale is needed for recipes, such as sauerkraut, that specify ingredients by weight. The weight measures are necessary to ensure correct proportions of salt to vegetable. For long-term storage, you will need a boiling-water bath canner and the appropriate jars and lids. (For more information see Canning, pages 40–51.)

Dill Pickles Whole cucumbers pickle well, but you may need to purchase very large jars.

PICKLING METHODS

There are several ways to pickle produce: fresh-pack, as chutneys or relishes, refrigerated, salt-brined, and frozen. All work as preserving techniques though each method can change the final flavor of the produce.

Method: Fresh-Pack Pickles

For details on the canning process, see Canning, pages 40–51.

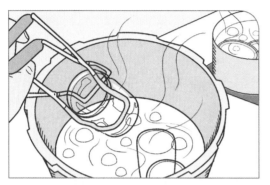

1 Prepare the canner, canning jars, and lids according to the instructions on page 46.

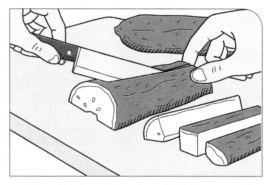

2 Assemble all your ingredients. Wash the vegetables and chop or slice as required.

3 Make up the vinegar brine according to the recipe; never reduce the amount of vinegar required. Heat to boiling.

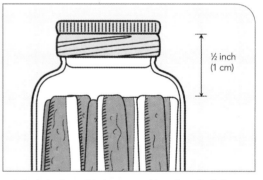

½ inch (1 cm)

4 Pack the jars with the vegetables, then the brine, leaving the proper amount of headspace as specified in the recipe, generally ½ inch (1 cm). Wipe each jar clean, then close the jars.

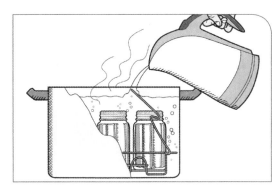

5 Process in a boiling-water bath for length of time the recipe specifies, usually 10 minutes for cucumber pickles in pint (500 ml) jars. Begin counting the time when the water returns to a boil.

6 When the processing time is up, remove the jars and place on a folded towel or wooden rack. Allow to cool for 24 hours, then check the seals (see page 50). For best flavor, allow the pickles to mature for 4–6 weeks before opening.

PICKLING THE PAST

- The ancient Mesopotamians made pickles as far back as 2400 B.C., according to archaeological evidence.
- Cleopatra attributed her good looks to pickles.
- Aristotle wrote about the healing effects of pickles.
- Julius Caesar made sure pickles were included in the diet of his soldiers.
- Shakespeare peppered his speeches with references to pickles, including "Oh, Hamlet, how camest thou in such a pickle?" (*Hamlet*, Act 5, Scene 1).
- Columbus brought the first cucumbers to the New World.
- In 1535 Jacques Cartier, a French explorer, found "very great cucumbers" grown on the site of what is now Montréal.
- Napoleon valued pickles as a healthy food for his armies and offered the equivalent of $250,000 to anyone who could figure out how to preserve food safely.
- Thomas Jefferson once wrote, "On a hot day in Virginia, I know nothing more comforting than a fine spiced pickle, brought up troutlike from the sparkling depths of the aromatic jar below the stairs of Aunt Sally's cellar."
- In 1858 John Mason designed and patented the first Mason jar, which was made of a heavier weight glass to withstand the high temperatures needed for pickle processing.
- During World War II, the U.S. government had to ration pickles, because 40 percent of the country's pickle production went to feed soldiers.
- Today about 5 million pounds (2,500,000 kg) of pickles are consumed annually in the United States. That's 9 pounds (4 kg) of pickles per American per year!

Method: Chutneys, Relishes, and Ketchup

For detailed instructions on the canning process, see Canning, pages 40–51.

1 Prepare the canner, canning jars, and lids according to the instructions on page 46.

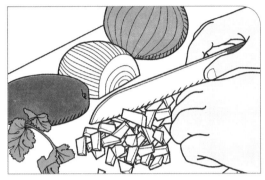

2 Assemble all your ingredients. Wash the vegetables and chop or slice as required.

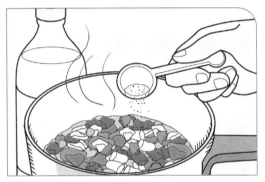

3 Combine the ingredients in a nonreactive saucepan and cook according to the recipe directions, adding as much sugar and vinegar as the recipe specifies.

½ inch (1 cm)

4 Pack the jars with the chutney or relish, leaving the amount of headspace specified in the recipe, generally ½ inch (1 cm). Wipe the rim clean on each, then close the jars.

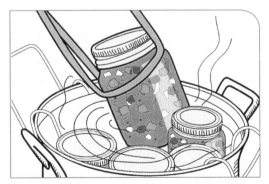

5 Process for length of time the recipe specifies, usually 10 minutes, counting from the time when the water returns to a boil.

6 When the processing time is up, remove the jars and place on a folded towel or wooden rack. Allow to cool for 24 hours, then check the seals (see page 50). For best flavor, allow chutneys and relishes to mature for 4–6 weeks before opening.

Zucchini Relish

Zucchini relish is a wonderful accompaniment for summer barbecues, especially on homemade beef burgers. It's also good on its own, or for breakfast with a poached egg!

2 tablespoons (12 g) salt

8 cups (800 g) chopped zucchini

1 cup (250 g) chopped onion

1½ cups (350 ml) white vinegar

2½ cups (500 g) sugar

2 teaspoons (10 ml) mustard seeds
   or Dijon mustard

1½ teaspoons (7 ml) celery seeds

1 Sprinkle the salt over the zucchini and the onions. Allow to set for 3 hours before draining well.

2 Mix together the vinegar, sugar, mustard seeds, and celery seeds in a saucepan and bring to a boil. Add the zucchini mixture to the saucepan.

3 Simmer for 20 minutes.

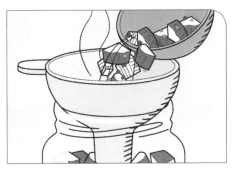

4 Pour the mixture into clean, hot jars, leaving ½ inch (1 cm) headspace. Process for 15 minutes in a boiling-water bath. Makes approximately 3 pints (1.5 L) zucchini relish.

Method: Salt-Brined Pickles

Salt-brined pickles are made from raw vegetables and salt, which acts as a preservative. The salt creates a brine by drawing liquid from the vegetables. With cucumbers, additional water is needed to make enough brine. Naturally occurring bacteria convert the sugars in the raw vegetables into lactic acid in a process known as lacto-fermentation. The lactic acid, which is smoother tasting than the acetic acid of vinegar, gives salt-cured pickles their distinctive flavor.

For successful salt-cured pickles, meticulous cleanliness is required to prevent undesirable bacteria and yeasts from colonizing the pickles before the fermentation process has been completed.

1 Prepare the crock by thoroughly washing with hot soapy water and rinsing well.

2 Prepare the vegetables by washing, then slicing or chopping as needed.

3 Pack the crock, leaving several inches (about 10 cm) at the top of the crock. For sauerkraut and similar recipes, layer the vegetables with a specified amount of salt, then tamp down on the layers as you pack to draw out liquid from the vegetables (see page 114). For cucumbers and other vegetables to which you add a salt brine, pack tightly, but do not tamp down.

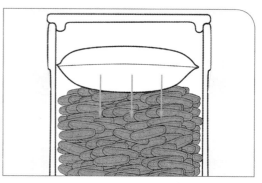

4 If you have not added a brine, wait a few hours for a brine to form. If the brine does not completely cover the vegetables, or if you are adding brine, pour the brine over the vegetables, being sure that the brine completely covers the vegetables. There needs to be about 4 inches (10 cm) of space over the top of the brine. Weight the vegetables with a zippered plastic bag filled with water to be sure that all of the vegetables are submerged under the brine and that air is excluded from the surface. It is alright if the bag bulges to the top of the crock. If your crock is not airtight, cover the entire crock with plastic wrap to prevent dust and airborne molds and yeasts from falling into the brine.

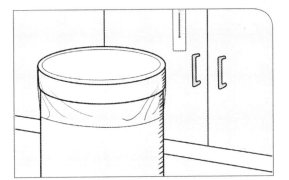

5 Store the crock at room temperature in a slightly cool spot; 70° F (20° C) is ideal. At colder temperatures, the fermentation process will take longer; at higher temperatures, the fermentation process will be more rapid.

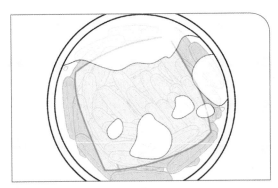

6 Check the crock daily and remove any scum that forms on top. Fermentation will begin in a few days. Watch for air bubbles escaping from the crock. At the end of 2–6 weeks, the pickles will be pleasantly sour. Refrigerate to halt the fermentation process.

7 For long-term storage, process in a boiling-water bath according to the instructions on page 46. If the brine is clear and tasty, pack the fermented vegetables in canning jars and top off with the brine. If the brine is cloudy or does not taste good, drain the pickles and pack in jars with fresh brine.

TROUBLESHOOTING

Soggy pickles have many causes. Overripe cucumbers or cucumbers that were not properly chilled after harvest could be the cause. With fresh-pack pickles, the cause may be vinegar that was too weak, water that was too hard, or storage that was too warm. With brined pickles, the cause could be insufficient salt, insufficient brine, or failure to slice off the blossom end.

ADJUSTING THE SALT

Your salt-cured pickles may taste too salty for your palate. Don't be tempted to reduce the amount of salt the recipe requires, because the salt acts as a preservative; instead, rinse the pickles in cool water until they taste just right before serving.

Method: Refrigerator and Freezer Pickles

Refrigerator pickling and freezer pickling are becoming increasingly popular ways to preserve, because they don't require canning or any special equipment.

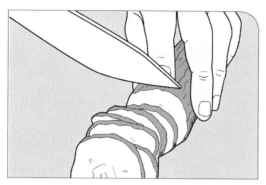

1 Wash and prepare the vegetables. Cucumbers need to be sliced very thinly to ensure a crisp texture.

2 Salt the vegetables to draw out excess moisture. Let drain in a colander for at least 30 minutes.

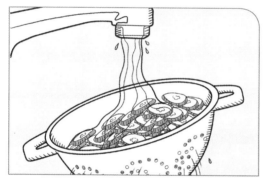

3 Rinse the vegetables until they taste pleasantly— not overly—salty.

4 Combine the ingredients to make a vinegar brine. Add to the vegetables.

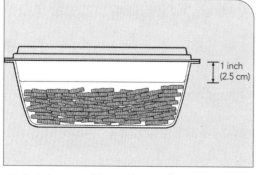

5 Pack the vegetables and brine in freezer containers, leaving a 1-inch (2.5-cm) headspace, and freeze.

6 Defrost overnight in the refrigerator before serving.

What Went Wrong?

If your pickle doesn't turn out as you had hoped, do not be discouraged. Follow the chart below to identify the cause of any pickling problems so you can fix them the next time around.

PROBLEM	POSSIBLE CAUSE(S)
Soft or slippery pickles	Not enough vinegar
	Storage area too warm
	Water too hard
Shriveled pickles	Cucumbers wilted at start
	Pickling brine too sweet
	Pickling brine has too much vinegar
Hollow pickles	Cucumbers had insufficient water while growing
	Cucumbers stored too long before pickling
Dark pickles	Minerals in water
	Copper, brass, galvanized, or iron cookware used
	Insufficient nitrogen levels in soil where cucumbers grew
Dull or faded pickles	Poor-quality cucumbers used
White sediment in jar	Table salt was used
Spoiled cucumbers	Jars not sterilized
	Jars not sealed
	Air not excluded from fermenting pickles

·BEETS·

Life—a spiritual pickle preserving the body from decay.

— Ambrose Bierce

Do You Relish Chutney?

Chutneys are tangy condiments for curries and roasted meats, perfect spreads for breads and lively partners to cheeses. These sweet and spicy relishes, called chatni in India, are often served as a condiment to add zing to blander foods, such as rice and breads. Chutneys are made with spices, vinegar, herbs, fruit, and vegetables in countless configurations.

Each region of India has its own specialties: Walnut chutneys are treasured in Kashmir; coconut chutneys are popular in the south; and tomato versions are made throughout the country. Other common ingredients include limes, apples, peaches, plums, apricots, and lemons. Additional spices may include cloves, garlic, cilantro, mustard, cinnamon, ginger, cayenne pepper, jalapeños, tamarind, and mint.

Tomato Chutney

Tomato chutney is traditionally enjoyed with cheese and cold meats. It also works well in sandwiches. You could try adding a fresh red or green chile, finely diced, with the seasonings to get a spicy tomato chutney that goes well with anything, even plain boiled rice. This is also a good recipe to use up unripened tomatoes: Replace ripe tomatoes with an equal quantity of unripened tomatoes, and add 10–15 minutes to the simmer time.

7 pounds (3 kg) ripe tomatoes
1 pound (450 g) onions
2 tablespoons (25 g) salt
2 teaspoons (10 ml) paprika

½ teaspoon (2–3 ml) cayenne pepper
1 cup (300 ml) malt vinegar
1¾ cups (350 g) sugar

1 Wash and chop the tomatoes, and peel and chop the onions.

2 Combine the tomatoes and onions in a heavy-bottomed saucepan, and simmer for 20–30 minutes until tender. Add the salt, paprika, cayenne, and half of the vinegar.

3 Cook gently for 45 minutes, or until it begins to thicken. Then add the sugar and remaining vinegar, stirring until fully dissolved.

4 Continue simmering until the mixture becomes thick, stirring occasionally. Pour the mixture into clean, hot pint (500-ml) jars, leaving ½ inch (1 cm) headspace. Process for 15 minutes in a boiling-water bath. Makes approximately 6 pints (3 L).

Piccallili

This recipe combines the crunchy texture of a cabbage relish with the spicy sweetness of chutney.

16 green tomatoes, diced

6 onions, diced

6 red bell peppers, diced

Kernels from 6 ears sweet corn

1 medium-size head cabbage, cored and thinly sliced

¼ cup (25 g) pickling salt

2 tablespoons (30 ml) prepared mustard

6 cups (1.5 L) cider vinegar

2½ cups (500 g) sugar

2 tablespoon (15 g) celery seeds

2 teaspoon (2 g) whole cloves

2 teaspoons (6 g) black peppercorns

2 bay leaves

2 teaspoons (5 g) powdered ginger

1½ teaspoons (4.5 g) tumeric

1 Combine all the vegetables in a large bowl. Mix in the salt and let stand overnight. Drain away the liquid that accumulates.

2 Combine the remaining ingredients in a large saucepan and whisk until well blended. Simmer for 10 minutes, then strain.

3 Combine the drained vegetables and brine in a large saucepan. Simmer for 10 minutes. Pack into clean, hot pint (500-ml) jars, leaving ½ inch (1 cm) headspace.

4 Process in a boiling-water bath for 10 minutes. Makes 6–8 pints (3–4 L).

Dilled Zucchini Pickles

Zucchini pickles are a delicious, slightly fancier alternative to regular pickles. They go well with any rich savory meat, either on a sandwich or as a relish or condiment for roasted chicken. This a great recipe to help use a summer glut of zucchini!

2 pounds (900 g) fresh zucchini, washed and thinly sliced

2 small onions, thinly sliced

¼ cup (40 g) pickling salt

2 cups (300 g) sugar

2 teaspoons (6 g) mustard seeds

1 teaspoon (3 g) celery seeds

1 teaspoon (3 g) dill seeds

3 cups (700 ml) white vinegar

2 garlic cloves, peeled

1 Place the zucchini and the onions in a bowl with the salt and just enough water to cover them. Let them stand for 2 hours before draining thoroughly.

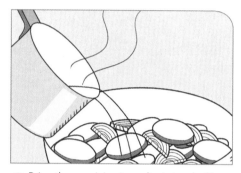

2 Bring the remaining ingredients to a boil in a pan. Then remove from the heat and pour the contents over the zucchini and onions. Let the new mixture stand for another 2 hours.

3 Return the mixture to the pan and allow to boil for 5 minutes.

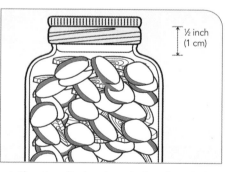

½ inch (1 cm)

4 Place 1 garlic clove in each clean, hot pint jar. Pack in the zucchini and brine, leaving ½ inch (1 cm) headspace. Process in a boiling-water bath for 15 minutes. Makes 2 pints (1 L).

Pickled Beets

If you have a large amount of beets that you want to store, pickling them is a fast and easy process that retains their flavor beautifully. Keep a damp cloth nearby at all times, and expect a few little purple stains here and there. Kitchen countertop stains can be prevented by wiping up any beet juices as soon as possible.

7 pounds (3.5 kg) fresh small beets,
    trimmed, leaving 1 inch stems and roots

8 small onions

8 whole cloves

4 cinnamon sticks, halved

4 cups (1 L) white vinegar

2 cups (500 ml) water

2 cups (400 g) sugar

2 tablespoons (20 g) pickling salt

1 Place the beets in a large saucepan and cover with water. Bring to a boil and boil until tender, about 15–25 minutes. Cool and peel.

2 Put 1 onion, 1 clove, and 1 piece of cinnamon stick in each clean, hot jar. Fill with the beets, leaving about ½ inch (1 cm) headspace.

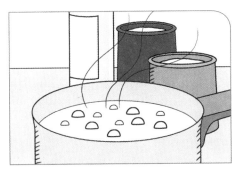

3 Combine the vinegar, water, sugar, and pickling salt in a saucepan and bring to a boil.

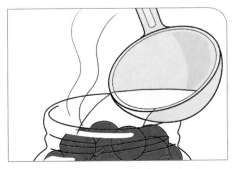

4 Pour the hot brine over the beets, leaving ½ inch (1 cm) headspace. Process for 30 minutes in a boiling-water bath. Makes 8 pints (4 L).

Dilly Beans

Dilly beans, or pickled green beans, take their name from the fact that they are often flavored strongly with dill. This is a great way to practice raw-pack canning, and the finished beans work well in salads or as an accompaniment to a main dish. Any type of green bean can be turned into dilly beans, but super-thin French-style beans stay tender and are less likely to be stringy or tough.

2 pounds (900 g) green beans, trimmed

1 tablespoon (6 g) crushed red pepper flakes (optional)

4 garlic cloves

4 fresh dill heads

¼ cup (40 g) salt

2½ cups (600 ml) white vinegar

2½ cups (600 ml) water

1 Pack the beans, lengthwise, into hot, sterilized jars, leaving ½ inch (1 cm) headspace. To each jar, add ¼ teaspoon (1 ml) red pepper flakes, 1 clove garlic, and 1 head dill.

2 Combine the remaining ingredients together in a pan and bring to a boil.

3 Pour, boiling hot, over the beans, leaving ½ inch (1 cm) headspace. Remove air bubbles with a chopstick. Seal caps.

4 Process for 5 minutes in a boiling-water bath. Makes 4 pints (2 L).

Red Onion Marmalade

Onion relishes have become very popular in recent years. Usually they are sweet-and-sour mixtures of slowly cooked onions designed to be served with sandwiches, steaks, and grilled meat. Try this marmalade with cheese and crackers, too.

¼ cup (60 ml) peanut oil
3 pounds (1.5 kg) red onions, some thinly
    sliced, some chopped
2 star anise, crushed
8 black peppercorns, crushed
1 teaspoon (2 g) salt

1 packed cup (200 g) light brown sugar,
    or 1 cup (190 g) granulated sugar
½ teaspoon (1.5 g) ground allspice
¾ cup (180 ml) raspberry vinegar
¾ cup (180 ml) sherry vinegar
¼ cup (60 ml) red wine vinegar

1 Heat the oil in a large skillet and add the onions, star anise, and peppercorns. Sprinkle with the salt, cover, and cook over low heat, stirring occasionally, until soft but not browned; the salt will draw out the water from the onions.

2 Stir in the sugar and allspice, and continue to cook for another 15 minutes, stirring occasionally.

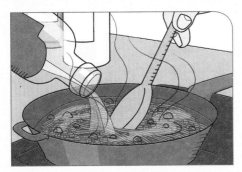

3 Pour in the vinegars and allspice and bring to a boil. Simmer gently until almost all the liquid has evaporated, stirring occasionally.

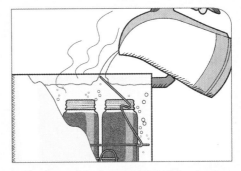

4 Pack into clean, hot pint (500-ml) jars, leaving ½ inch (1 cm) headspace. Process in a boiling-water bath for 10 minutes. Makes about 2 pints.

Ketchup

Ketchup is used internationally, and most people have a favorite brand or particular taste they enjoy the most. Now you can make your own ketchup using freshly harvested tomatoes and customize your very own flavors, changing the salt level or adding a little spice. In the middle of the winter, you can pour the ketchup on your plate and taste the summer-fresh tomatoes.

24 pounds (11 kg) fresh tomatoes
3 medium white onions, diced
1 clove garlic, minced
1 cup (240 g) sugar
1 teaspoon (5 ml) salt

1 teaspoon (5 ml) black pepper, finely ground
1 tablespoon (15 ml) celery seeds
3 cups (700 ml) cider vinegar

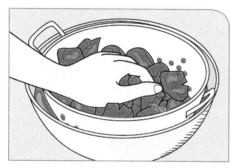

1 Seed and skin the tomatoes, and then squeeze out the water, using your hands. Drain the tomatoes in a sieve or colander, and catch the fresh juice for drinking. Empty the drained tomatoes into a large pot.

2 To the tomatoes, add the onions, garlic, sugar, salt, and black pepper. Bring to a boil, reduce the heat, and simmer for 45 minutes. Pass through a food mill or sieve.

3 Place celery seeds in the center of a square of cheesecloth. Tie the corners of the cloth together to make a little bag, and put the bag into a small saucepan with cider vinegar. Let it simmer for 30 minutes while the tomatoes cook in a separate pan. Remove the bag from the vinegar and add the seasoned vinegar to the tomato mixture. Cook down to thicken.

4 Pour into clean, hot pint (500-ml) jars, leaving ¼ inch (.5 cm) headspace. Process for 15 minutes in a boiling-water bath. Makes about 8 pints (4 L).

Freezer Bread-and-Butter Pickles

Requiring virtually no labor and absolutely no cooking time, freezer bread-and-butter pickles are perfect for the busy preserver. Just make sure to have enough room in the freezer and refrigerator.

4 cucumbers, thinly sliced

3 medium white onions, diced

2 green bell peppers, diced

Salt

2 cups (400 g) sugar

1 cup (240 ml) white vinegar

1 tablespoon (15 ml) mustard seeds

1 tablespoon (15 ml) celery seeds

1 In a bowl, combine cucumbers, onions, and green peppers. Sprinkle with salt, and let stand for 1 hour.

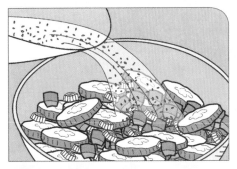

2 In another bowl, combine sugar, white vinegar, mustard seeds, and celery seeds, and pour this over the cucumber mixture. Refrigerate for 1 day.

3 Place the mixture in freezer containers, leaving 1 inch (2.5 cm) of headspace.

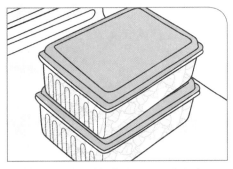

4 Freeze. This yields about 4 pints (2 L) of pickles. To serve, thaw in refrigerator for 6 hours.

Sauerkraut

Sauerkraut is often overlooked in terms of its nutritional value. However, it is a delicious, healthful side dish that fully deserves its place in your pantry.

5 pounds (2½ kg) shredded cabbage
3 tablespoons (45 g) pickling salt

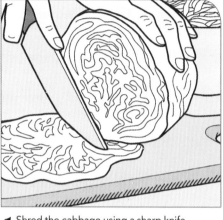

1 Shred the cabbage using a sharp knife.

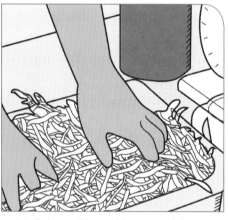

2 Wash thoroughly in cold water, and drain.

3 Place the shredded cabbage into a large crock. Mix the cabbage and salt with your hands.

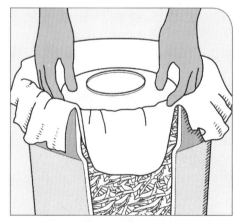

4 Pack gently with your hands or a potato masher until crock is nearly full. Cover with a cloth, a plate, and something heavy.

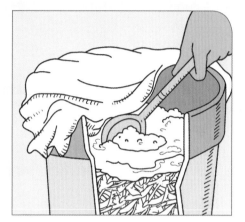

5 During the curing process, kraut needs daily attention. Strenuously tamp down on the cabbage to draw out the brine, and add salted water daily as needed for the cloth to remain moist.

6 Remove scum as it forms, and wash and scald the cloth often in order to keep it free of scum and mold.

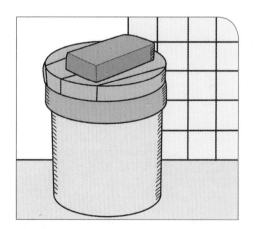

7 At room temperature, fermentation will be complete in 10–12 days. The finished sauerkraut can be kept tightly covered in the refrigerator for several months, or it can be canned. To can, pack clean hot quart (1 L) jars with the kraut and brine, leaving ½ inch (1 cm headspace). Process for 25 minutes in a boiling-water bath. Makes 2 to 3 quarts.

JAMS, JELLIES, AND BUTTERS

A pantry filled with jewel-like jars of jellies, jams (which are often called preserves), conserves, marmalades, and butters is a tasty tribute to the fruits of summer that will last throughout the winter. Homemade jams and jellies also make attractive gifts. Who isn't happy to receive a colorful jar of edible summer? There are several methods for making preserves, ranging from time-intensive and slightly unpredictable to quick, easy, and painless. Each technique results in a different flavor and texture, but there is a certain satisfaction to making preserves "the old-fashioned way."

Homemade jams and jellies taste more like fruit than store-bought ones, especially if you make them without commercial pectins, by cooking down fruit to its very essence. The amount of sweetener you add will be up to you. There are tips and hints that will allow you to make wonderful preserves that reflect your taste preferences and your style of cooking. Whether you want to make a traditional grape jelly for everyday peanut butter and jelly sandwiches or you want to spice up your strawberry preserves, this chapter will help you find your own signature recipe.

THE ROUTE FROM FRUIT TO FANTASTIC PRESERVES

In order to turn fresh, juicy fruit into something spreadable on toast, you must cook the fruit for a long time to evaporate much of the liquid. A quicker method is to combine the fruit with pectin, a naturally occurring substance that is found in many ripe fruits, especially apples, and cook briefly.

MAKING YOUR OWN JAMS AND JELLIES

The most labor-intensive way to make jams and jellies is the old-fashioned way—to cook the fruit or fruit juice until it gels. It also results in jams and jellies that taste intensely of fruit. The second most labor-intensive method of making jams and jellies is to use commercial pectin. This requires you to measure accurately and time carefully. In the end, you will have a jam or jelly with great consistency, but it may (or may not) require more sugar than you might want to use. If you follow the directions on the box of pectin faithfully, it is a pretty foolproof method. Either way, after you've made the preserves, they should be processed in a boiling-water bath for longer-term storage. By far the easiest way to make jams and jellies is to make freezer jams or jellies using pectin specially formulated for that process. There isn't much cooking

Making It Easy:
Make Preserves When
the Weather Is Cold

Don't feel like slaving over a hot stove in the heat of summer? Freeze your fruit (see Freezing, pages 30–39) until the weather turns cold. Then make preserves from fruit frozen without sugar; you won't be able to taste the difference.

Strawberry Preserves The strawberry is the first fruit of summer. You can preserve its flavor in a jar as a jam, jelly, or preserve.

involved, so the preserves taste very fresh. The preserves are stored in the freezer, so there is no need to process in a boiling-water bath canner.

Ingredients

Choosing your ingredients for making jams and jellies depends on how much time you want to spend cooking and your level of expertise. Some traditionalists see the use of commercial pectin as cheating, but it is more of a foolproof way to ensure good results.

Fruit The primary ingredient in jams and jellies is fruit. It doesn't have to be picture-perfect, but it must be free from mold or any spoilage. Wash the fruit and cut it up as specified in the recipe. Frozen or canned fruit can be used.

Pectin Pectin occurs naturally in fruit. Most apples, grapes, blueberries, blackberries, cranberries, and cherries have enough pectin that added pectin isn't necessary to make preserves with them. Other fruits are more easily made into preserves with the addition of pectin, which comes in both liquid and powdered form. When using commercial pectin, it is important that you follow the recipes from the manufacturer; commercial pectins are not interchangeable.

Sweeteners White sugar is used to sweeten most preserves. If you are using commercial pectin, you must use the exact amount of white sugar required. If you are making a jam or jelly without added pectin, you can sweeten to taste or use honey. Some sugar is needed to form a solid gel. Also sugar is a preservative; low-sugar jams and jellies spoil quickly once opened, even if refrigerated.

Acid To activate the pectin and contribute flavor, acid is usually required. Most recipes call for a small amount of lemon juice; do not omit.

> ## WHAT'S IN A NAME?
>
> Basically, fruit may be transformed into six different types of gelled fruit products.
>
> - **Jelly** Clear fruit juice that is cooked to hold its shape on a spoon but is spreadable on toast.
> - **Jam** Crushed or chopped fruit that is cooked to become a thick spread.
> - **Preserves** Small pieces of fruit that are suspended in clear, gelled syrup.
> - **Conserves** Jams made with combinations of fruit. They may contain nuts.
> - **Marmalades** Soft fruit jellies that contain small pieces of fruit.
> - **Butters** Fruit purées that are cooked down to a spreading consistency. They may or may not have added sugar.

Gifts from the Kitchen
Who isn't happy to receive a delicious jar of preserved summer fruit?

Ingredients Look for low-sugar pectins if you want to reduce the amount of added sugar in your recipes.

·JAM·

The rule is jam
tomorrow and jam
yesterday, but never
jam today.

—Lewis Carroll
(Charles Lutwidge Dodgson)

EQUIPMENT AND SUPPLIES

- Boiling-water bath canner
- Canning jars and lids
- Tall, heavy, nonreactive pot
- Food mill or strainer
- Steam juicer or jelly bag
- Candy thermometer
- Timer

Equipment

Jams and jellies are preserved for long-term storage by processing in a boiling-water bath or by freezing. In addition to the equipment needed for canning or freezing, you will need the following equipment.

- Tall, heavy pot. Jams and jellies must boil vigorously as they cook. To reduce the chance they will boil over, height is required. Use nonreactive pots—nothing made of aluminum, brass, galvanized steel, or iron.

- A candy thermometer is needed to tell you when the gel point is reached if you are making a jam or jelly without commercial pectin.

- A steam juicer or jelly bag (available at most specialty kitchen stores) is needed for extracting fruit juices to make jelly.

- A boiling-water bath canner for long-term storage.

- Usually ½-pint (250-ml) jars are used to make preserves.

Low-Sugar Preserves

If diabetes means you or a friend or family member cannot eat delicious homemade jams and jellies, you can make low-sugar preserves via a few different routes. Keep in mind, however, that sugar is necessary to preserves both as a preservative and for texture. Low-sugar jams have a very short shelf life. Once a jar is open, it must be refrigerated and used within a week. Also keep in mind that fruit is naturally high in fructose, and the amount of fructose becomes concentrated as the fruit cooks down.

There are specially formulated "low-sugar pectins" available in health-food stores. Follow the directions on the package for best results; these products yield better results when you are able to add sweeteners to taste. Preserves made from high-pectin fruit will gel when the mixture reaches 220° F (105° C), without the addition of any sugar. The fruit will be very concentrated in flavor. You can experiment with adding sugar substitutes that are formulated for baking.

History

The earliest written records of jams and jellies in Western Europe date back to the first crusade in 1095. Returning knights brought fruit spreads back from the Middle East, and this international method of preserving has gained in popularity ever since. The process of boiling the sealed jars in water was published in 1810 by French confectioner Nicolas Appert; jams and jellies lasted even longer once this idea gained momentum. The method is mostly unchanged, though the invention of home freezers has allowed for some quicker and less messy preserve recipes.

Preserving was a home-based activity well into the 1900s. In 1897 Jerome Smucker, whose name is associated with a very famous brand of fruit preserves, constructed a cider mill in Ohio, where he made apple butter from some of the cider he produced. By 1900 Smucker and his son, Willard, were traveling across northeastern Ohio, selling their products. In 1921 the J. M. Smucker Company officially formed and, in 1923, it began to produce additional jams and jellies besides just apple butter. By 1935 the J. M. Smucker Company's products were in great demand across the Midwest and were selling nationwide by 1942. The same thing happened to Dr. Thomas Branwell Welch of Massachusetts, who popularized the delicious Concord grape in his first jam product, which was released in 1923. This spread was so popular that the U.S. Army purchased Welch's entire inventory.

Considering they are delicious and relatively easy to make, the future of jams, jellies, and preserves is clear. As part of the culinary heritage of many nations, preserves will continue to be manufactured professionally and made by jam enthusiasts at home. New flavors will emerge, such as the already popular hot-pepper jelly, and people all over the world will enjoy jams, jellies, and preserves for a long time to come.

TESTING FOR DONENESS WITHOUT A THERMOMETER

The trickiest part of making jams and jellies without added pectin is judging when the preserves are done. A reliable candy thermomenter will tell you when: at 220° F (105° C).

Your grandmother probably used to test jams and jellies for doneness using the "sheet test." Dip a metal spoon into the boiling fruit mixture and lift the spoon out of the steam so the syrup runs off the side. When the mixture first starts to boil, the drops will be light and syrupy. As the mixture continues to boil, the drops become heavier and will drop off the spoon two at a time. When the two drops form together and "sheet" off the spoon, the gel point has been reached.

Alternatively, drop a small amount of the fruit mixture onto a plate and place the plate in the freezer for a few minutes. If the mixture gels, it is done. During this test, the rest of the mixture needs to be removed from the heat to prevent overcooking.

If you remove your preserves before it reaches gel point, the preserves will be runny. You can boil it again, or simply call it "syrup" and serve it over ice cream!

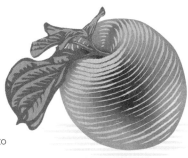

Apricots These fruits make delicious preserves, but they always require added pectin to get the right consistency.

Method: Making Jams, Preserves, and Conserves without Pectin

This method of making preserves without added pectin is suitable for all sorts of fruits, though some fruits are naturally higher in pectin than others (see page 125). The lower the natural pectin in the fruit, the longer it will take for the fruit to reach its gel point and the more concentrated your preserve will be.

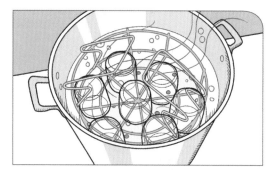

1 Prepare the canner, canning jars, and lids according to the instructions on page 46. Jars need to be sterilized if the processing time is less than 10 minutes.

2 Wash the fruit and prepare according to the recipe directions, for example by crushing, chopping, or slicing.

3 Combine the fruit, sugar, and lemon juice in a tall, heavy pot, and cook over low heat until the sugar dissolves. Bring to a boil, and stir frequently until the mixture begins to thicken.

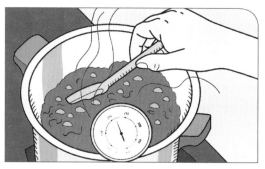

4 Continue to boil until the mixture reaches 220° F (105° C) on a candy thermometer.

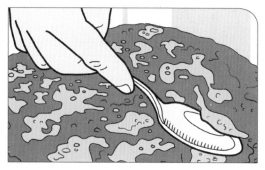

5 Remove from the heat and skim off any foam that has formed on top.

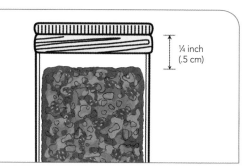

¼ inch
(.5 cm)

6 Pack into jars, leaving the amount of headspace specified in the recipe, usually ¼ inch (.5 cm) for ½-pint (250-ml) jars. Wipe the rims clean, then close the jars.

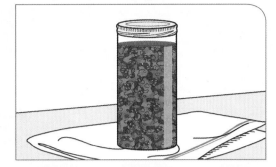

7 Process in a boiling-water bath for the length of time the recipe specifies, usually 10 minutes for a ½-pint (250-ml) jar. Begin counting the time when the water returns to a boil.

8 When the processing time is up, remove the jars and place on a folded towel or wooden rack. Allow to cool for 24 hours, then check the seals (see page 50).

Very Berry Jam

Raspberries are low in pectin, while red currants are a rich source. Combining them not only makes a delicious jam but also solves any setting problems.

2 pounds (900 g) raspberries
1 pound (450 g) red currants, stripped from their stalks
Juice of 1 lemon
7 cups (1.25 kg) granulated sugar
Pat of butter (optional)

Prepare your canner, canning jars, and lids according to the instructions on page 46. Put half the raspberries and all the red currants in a nonreactive pan and cook over very low heat until the juices run, stirring gently, if necessary. Add the remaining raspberries, lemon juice, and sugar to the pan. Heat gently, stirring, to dissolve the sugar, then increase the heat and boil until the fruit reaches its gel point at 220 °F (105 °C). Add the butter if scum formation is a problem. Remove from the heat. Fill the jars, leaving headspace of ¼ inch (.5 cm), and process in a boiling-water bath for 10 minutes. Let cool, label the jars, and store in a cool, dark, dry place for up to 1 year.
Makes about 6 ½-pint (250-ml) jars

Blackberry and Apple Jam with Cardamom

Blackberry and apple go together so well they seem to be a natural partnership. The cardamom adds a rich warmth and depth of flavor.

¾ pound (350 g) tart apples, peeled, cored, and diced
⅔ cup (150 ml) water
2 pounds (950 g) blackberries
3 cups (575 g) sugar
Seeds from 3 cardamom pods, lightly crushed
Half a lemon, juiced

Prepare your canner, canning jars, and lids according to the instructions on page 46. Put the apples and water in a tall, heavy pot; bring to a boil on high heat; then reduce heat and simmer for about 15 minutes until the apples are soft. Add the blackberries and sugar and cook gently for a few minutes until they are soft and the sugar is dissolved. Tie the cardamom seeds in a cheesecloth bag and add to the pan with the lemon juice. Bring to a boil and boil until the fruit reaches its gel point at 220 °F (105 °C). Scoop out and discard the spice bag. Fill the jars, leaving a headspace of ¼ inch (.5 cm), and process in a boiling-water bath for 10 minutes. Remove and let cool, label the jars, and store in a cool, dark, dry place for up to 1 year.
Makes about 6 ½-pint (250-ml) jars

Peach Conserve

This recipe puts bruised or slightly imperfect fruit to good use. Use a good-quality brandy because its taste will be reflected in the conserve.

About 2½ pounds (1.1 kg) peaches
Juice of 2 lemons
3 cups (575 g) granulated sugar
Small pat of unsalted butter
¼ cup brandy
1–2 vanilla beans, cut into 3-inch lengths

Prepare your canner, canning jars, and lids according to the instructions on page 46. Dip each peach in boiling water for 30 seconds, then peel off the skin. Cut the peaches in half; remove the pits and any bruised flesh. Chop the peaches. Put the peaches in a nonreactive pan with the lemon juice and sugar. Cover and leave for a few hours, stirring occasionally. Add the butter and boil hard, stirring frequently, until the fruit reaches its gel point at 220 °F (105 °C). Remove from the heat and leave for 10 minutes. Stir in the brandy. Fill the prepared jars, inserting a piece of vanilla in each one, and leaving headspace of ¼ inch (.5 cm). Process in a boiling-water bath for 10 minutes. Remove and let cool, label the jars and store in a cool, dark, dry place for up to 1 year.
Makes about 4 ½-pint (250-ml) jars

Method: Making Jams, Preserves, and Conserves with Pectin

These are general directions. For best results, follow the exact recipe on the pectin package.

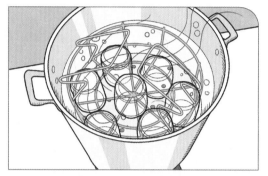

1 Prepare the canner, canning jars, and lids according to the instructions on page 46. Jars should be sterilized if the processing time is less than 10 minutes.

2 Wash the fruit and prepare according to the recipe directions by crushing, chopping, or slicing.

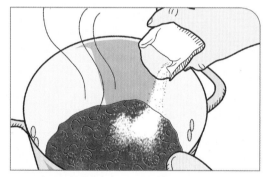

3 Combine the fruit and lemon juice in a tall, heavy pot. Add the pectin and bring to a full rolling boil that cannot be stirred down. Add the sugar, return to a boil, and boil for exactly 1 minute.

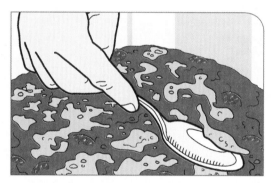

4 Remove from the heat and skim off any foam that has formed on top.

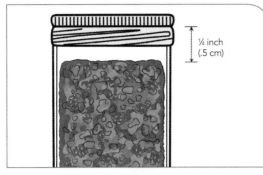

¼ inch
(.5 cm)

5 Pack into jars, leaving the amount of headspace specified in the recipe, usually ¼ inch (.5 cm) for ½-pint (250-ml) jars. Wipe the rims clean, then close the jars.

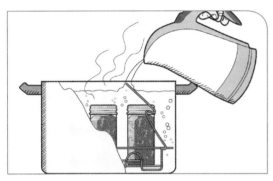

6 Process in a boiling-water bath for the length of time the recipe specifies, usually 5 minutes for ½-pint (250-ml) jars. Begin counting the time when the water returns to a boil.

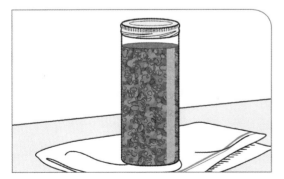

7 When the processing time is up, remove the jars and place on a folded towel or wooden rack. Allow to cool for 24 hours, then check the seals (see page 50).

PECTIN IN FRUIT

Pectin concentrations in fruit vary. The pectin content in all fruit is also generally higher when fruit is barely ripe, and diminishes as it matures from fully ripe to overripe. The process of ripening involves the breakdown of pectins, which softens the fruit as it ripens. Apples and crabapples (especially unripe ones) are good sources of pectin and are often used in making commercial pectin. Some commercial pectin is made from citrus peels.

- **Fruits High in Pectin** Citrus peel—but not the fruit of—oranges, tangerines grapefruit, and lemons; wild grapes (Eastern Concord variety); cranberries; gooseberries; boysenberries; blackberries; currants; loganberries; most Japanese plums; quinces

- **Fruits with Moderate Levels of Pectin** Ripe apples, very ripe blackberries, sour cherries, chokecherries, elderberries, grapefruit, bottled grape juice (Eastern Concord), oranges, rhubarb

- **Fruits Low in Pectin** Apricots, blueberries, sweet cherries, sour cherries, figs, grapefruit, grape juice, grapes (other than wild and Concord types), melons, oranges, pears, Italian plums, raspberries, strawberries

- **Fruits Very Low in Pectin** Nectarines, peaches, elderberries

Citrus The peels of fruits such as oranges and lemons are high in pectin.

Jams, Jellies, and Butters **125**

Method: Making Jelly without Pectin

Use at least one part underripe fruit to three parts just-ripe fruit to ensure sufficient naturally occurring pectin to gel.

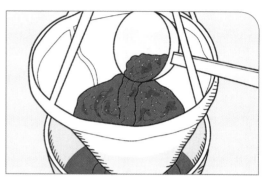

1 To extract the fruit juice, wash the fruit. Chop as needed, but do not peel. Put the fruit in a heavy pot. Add just enough water to prevent scorching. Crush soft fruits to get the juices flowing. Cook for about 30 minutes, until the fruit is completely tender.

2 Pour the fruit mixture into a damp jelly bag or colander lined with a double thickness of cheesecloth set over a bowl, and allow the fruit juice to collect overnight. Do not press on the fruit if you want a clear jelly.

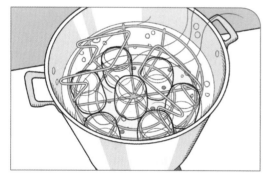

3 Prepare the canner, canning jars, and lids according to the instructions on page 46. Jars should be sterilized if the processing time is less than 10 minutes.

4 Working with up to 4 cups (950 ml) of juice at a time, add ¾ cup (150 g) sugar for each cup of juice and combine in a tall pot. Add lemon juice as specified in the recipe. Cook over low heat until the sugar is dissolved. Bring to a boil, then stir frequently until the mixture reaches 220° F (105° C) on a candy thermometer.

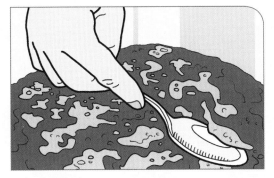

5 Remove from the heat and skim off any foam that has formed on top.

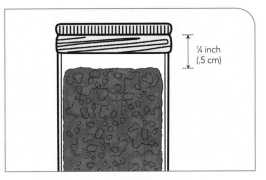

¼ inch
(.5 cm)

6 Pack into jars, leaving the amount of headspace specified in the recipe, usually ¼ inch (.5 cm) for ½-pint (250-ml) jars. Wipe the rims clean, then close the jars.

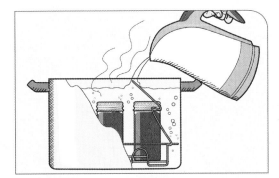

7 Process ½-pint (250-ml) jars for 5 minutes in the boiling-water bath (see page 47 for instructions), counting the time from when the water returns to a boil.

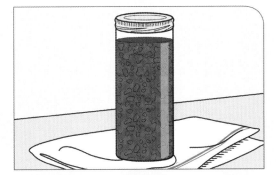

8 When the processing time is up, remove the jars and place on a folded towel or wooden rack. Allow to cool for 24 hours, then check the seals (see page 50).

Method: Making Jelly with Pectin

These are general directions. For best results, follow the exact recipe on the pectin package.

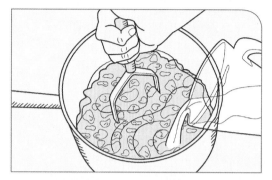

1 To extract the fruit juice, first wash the fruit. Chop as needed, but do not peel. Put the fruit in a heavy pot. Add just enough water to prevent scorching. Crush soft fruits to get the juices flowing. Cook for about 30 minutes, until the fruit is completely tender.

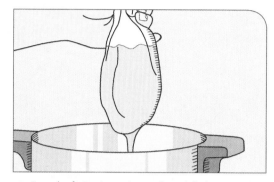

2 Pour the fruit mixture into a damp jelly bag or colander lined with a double thickness of cheesecloth set over a bowl, and allow the fruit juice to collect overnight. Do not press on the fruit if you want a clear jelly.

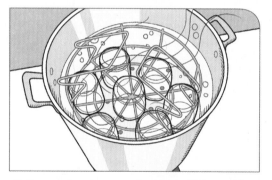

3 Prepare the canner, canning jars, and lids according to the instructions on page 46. Jars should be sterilized if the processing time is less than 10 minutes.

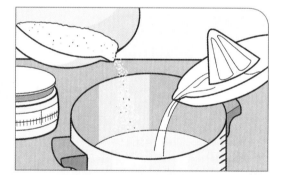

4 Mix the juice and pectin in a tall, heavy pot. Bring to a boil, add the sugar and lemon juice, and return to a boil. Boil for 1 minute, stirring constantly.

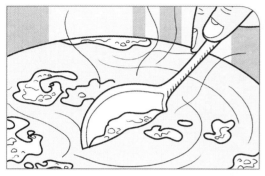

5 Remove from the heat and skim off any foam that has formed on top.

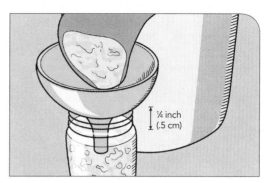

¼ inch
(.5 cm)

6 Pack into jars, leaving the amount of headspace specified in the recipe, usually ¼ inch (.5 cm) for ½-pint (250-ml) jars. Wipe the rims clean, then close the jars.

7 Process ½-pint (250 ml) jars in a boiling-water bath for 5 minutes, counting the time from after the water has returned to a boil.

8 When the processing time is up, remove the jars and place on a folded towel or wooden rack. Allow to cool for 24 hours, then check the seals (see page 50).

FREEZER JAMS AND JELLIES

Making jam can be an ambitious undertaking in the midst of the summer heat. However, freezer jam is a refreshing solution. It is easy and safe and tastes remarkably like fresh fruit since the jam is never cooked.

Preparation

Before you start making your freezer jams and jellies, be sure to have your containers ready and waiting. Use either sturdy plastic containers with tight-fitting lids or short, wide-mouthed glass jars made especially for the freezer. It's a good idea to choose containers that are no bigger than pints; the jam will not set up as well in larger containers. And you can wash them as you would any other dishes because there's no need to boil them as required with boiling-water bath canning.

Ingredients

The ingredients for freezer jams and jellies are few, but it's vital to follow your recipe exactly if you want delicious results.

Fruit Use perfectly ripe fruit. Since you won't be cooking it, the flavor of the jam or jelly is going to match the fruit. Therefore, if the fruit is over- or underripe, you'll be able to taste it.

Pectin Because freezer jam is not cooked, most recipes call for additional pectin to thicken it. Commercially produced pectin is derived from fruit. Store-bought pectin comes in two forms: powder and liquid. These are not interchangeable: use whichever form the recipe requires. Most common freezer jams call for powdered pectin. The basic ratios for each packet of powdered pectin are: 3 cups mashed fruit, 5 cups sugar, 1 cup water to dissolve and boil the pectin. The instructions can vary depending on the brand of pectin, so be sure to follow the directions on the packet.

Sugar This important ingredient inhibits the growth of bacteria. Jam recipes are formulated to call for a certain ratio of pectin to sugar, and they will not jell properly if you do not use the correct amount.

Storage

As the name implies, freezer jam is meant to be stored in the freezer. In fact, it will keep beautifully in the freezer for up to a year or in the refrigerator for up to 3 weeks. Once you open a container of jam, be sure to keep it refrigerated and use it within 3 weeks.

MAKING FREEZER JELLY AND JAM WITH CHILDREN

Making jam can be time-consuming, and it deals with boiling liquids and large, heavy pots. Although you may want to teach your children about preserving fruit, the long process involved to make and can homemade preserves might not hold their attention. Freezer jam is a fun way around this problem, and it avoids putting young children in harm's way.

Method: Making Freezer Jams and Jellies

These are general directions. Buy pectin that is specially formulated to make freezer jams and jellies and follow the recipes on the pectin package. Because the fruit is usually not cooked in this method, freezer jams have a distinctively fresh fruit flavor when compared to traditionally made jams.

1 Prepare the fruit juice or fruit as desired.

2 Combine the fruit, sugar, and acid as required in the recipe.

3 Dissolve the pectin in water in a small pot and bring to a boil. Boil for 1 minute.

4 Add the pectin to fruit and sugar and stir for about 3 minutes.

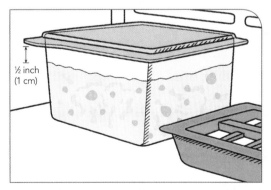

½ inch (1 cm)

5 Pour into freezer containers, leaving at least ½ inch (1 cm) of headspace. Let stand until set, up to 24 hours. Freeze for long-term storage.

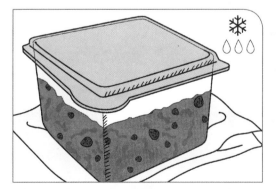

6 Defrost overnight in the refrigerator before serving. Never refreeze leftovers, but refrigerate for up to a week.

Method: Making Fruit Butters

Fruit butters are an excellent, economical way of preserving a harvest—though they may be labor-intensive to produce, they use very little sugar and will keep a lot longer than regular preserves. The term "butter" refers to the consistency of the finished preserve rather than the involvement of any dairy. Apple butter is the most famous, but most fruits make good butters.

1 Prepare the fruit according to the recipe. Generally you can simply halve or quarter the fruit and cook with the skins on or off.

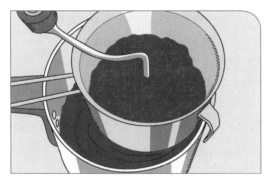

2 If fruit has the skin on, cook on top of the stove with just enough water or liquid to prevent scorching, until completely tender. Pass through a food mill to remove skins. If fruit is peeled, cook with just enough water or liquid to prevent scorching until the fruit is tender.

3 Continue to cook on top of the stove, stirring frequently until the fruit has cooked down to a spreadable consistency. This process will take several hours. Alternatively, transfer the fruit to a 200° F (90° C) oven and bake, stirring occasionally, for up to 8 hours.

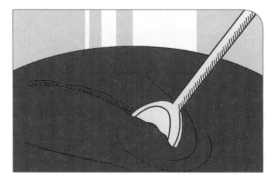

4 The butter is done when it will hold the trail of a spoon that is drawn through it.

5 Sweeten to taste with sugar, honey, corn syrup, or maple syrup. Add spices such as cinnamon, if desired.

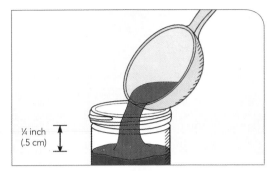

6 Pack into jars, leaving the amount of headspace specified in the recipe, usually ¼ inch (.5 cm) for ½-pint (250-ml) jars. Wipe the rims clean and close the jars.

7 Process ½-pint (250-ml) jars in a boiling-water bath for 5 minutes (see page 47), counting the time from after the water has returned to a boil.

¼ inch
(.5 cm)

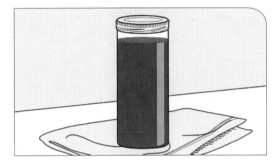

8 When the processing time is up, remove the jars and place on a folded towel or wooden rack. Allow to cool for 24 hours, then check the seals (see page 50).

Spiced Apple Butter

The quantities given in this recipe work well without the spices, but spread the spiced apple butter on toast, and you have an instant hit of apple pie! Apple butter will keep for several weeks.

6 pounds (2.75 kg) apples
2 pints (1 L) water
2 pints (1 L) cider
Sugar
1 teaspoon (5 g) ground cinnamon
1 teaspoon (5 g) ground cloves
½ teaspoon (2.5 g) ground allspice
Zest of ½ lemon, grated finely

Wash the apples and cut into pieces. Place in a stainless steel or enameled pan with the water and cider. Bring to a boil, then simmer until the apples are very soft. Pass through a food mill to remove skins. Return to the pan and simmer until it has reduced and is thick. Stir in sugar to taste. Add the cinnamon, cloves, allspice, and lemon zest. Cook, stirring, until the mixture is so thick it holds the trail of the spoon. Pack into sterilized hot ½-pint jars and process in a boiling-water bath (see page 47) for 5 minutes. Store in a cool, dry place.
Makes about 8 ½-pint (250 ml) jars

Apricot–Orange Butter

Orange rind and juice enhance the flavor of the apricots in this recipe. For a special treat and an even more pronounced apricot flavor, add 2–4 tablespoons (30–60 ml) apricot liqueur just before the end of the cooking.

3 pounds (1.5 kg) ripe apricots, halved and pitted
2 oranges, zested and juiced
Water
Sugar

Put the apricots, orange rind, and orange juice in a nonreactive pan and add enough water to just cover. Simmer gently, uncovered, for about 45 minutes, stirring occasionally with a wooden spoon, until the fruit is very soft. Remove from the heat. Pass through a food mill into a clean pan. For each 2½ cups (600 ml) purée, add 1¾ cups (350 g) sugar and heat gently, stirring, until the sugar has dissolved. Bring to a boil over a high heat and boil rapidly for 30–40 minutes, stirring frequently, until the mixture is thick. Remove from heat. Pack into sterilized hot ½-pint jars and process in a boiling-water bath (see page 47) for 5 minutes. Store in a cool dry place.
Makes about 6 ½-pint (250 ml) jars

JUICES, SOFT DRINKS, AND LIQUEURS

G arden fruits and vegetables can be used to make delicious juices, soft drinks, and liqueurs. The process is easier than you might think, and very economical. Traditional liqueurs and flavored vodkas are perfect for entertaining, and everyone is always impressed when you tell them they're homemade. While there is specialized equipment you can buy for each process—juicers can be very expensive—the results are just as delicious when made by hand, and your choice will be governed by whether you want to spend time or money making the end product.

There are various techniques for creating your own soft drinks, ranging from the traditional combination with baking soda to a quick-and-easy modern technique of adding store-bought ingredients to your homemade juice. Homemade liqueurs, using the crops from your kitchen garden, are very easy and require hardly any labor. Try the recipes in this chapter to decide on your favorite flavors, and enjoy the fruits of summer preserved long into the winter.

MAKING HOMEMADE BEVERAGES

There's something incredibly satisfying about making beverages, especially if some of the ingredients come fresh from your garden. Your family and friends can enjoy homemade juices, wine, beer, liqueurs, and naturally flavored vodkas at the next holiday gathering.

JUICES

Homemade juices are delicious and nutritious. There is nothing so tasty as sitting down to breakfast with freshly juiced homegrown produce from the garden. Packed with vitamins and minerals, the juice can be frozen easily in containers for enjoying as beverages or turned into sorbets.

Handling Fruits and Vegetables

Before juicing, all fruits and vegetables need to be washed and cut into small pieces, if large. Hard or fibrous vegetables, such as carrots, beets, or celery, need to be briefly cooked, with just enough liquid to prevent scorching, until soft.

Equipment

There are dozens of different juice extractors available, and many manufacturers make claims about the health benefits of juice derived from their particular machines. Some extract juice by masticating the fruit, some using centrifugal force, and some by crushing, then pressing (twin gear or triturating). Each type of machine has its own pros and cons, including cost, ease of cleanup, efficiency of operation, and quality of end product.

Before buying a juicer, you should know that juice has been made without expensive gadgets for centuries. All you really need is a variety of common kitchen tools, such as a blender, potato masher, citrus reamer, colander, and food mill. You may also need a sieve or jelly bag to separate the juice from the pulp.

Preserving Juice

Fruit and tomato juices can be heated to boiling, then processed in a boiling-water bath. Other vegetable juices, such as carrot, should be pressure-canned. Or the juice can be frozen; be sure to leave plenty of headspace because the juice will expand as it freezes.

Methods: Extracting Juice

There are several methods to extract juice, and which one you choose depends on how much money you would like to spend. Sometimes juicing completely by hand can be the most rewarding method.

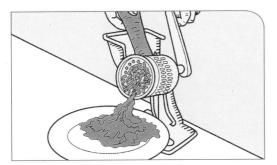

1 **Grind, chop, or purée.** Use a blender, food processor, food mill, or hand-cranked food grinder to reduce the fruit or vegetables to a pulp. Then drain the juice, straining through a sieve or jelly bag. To get a little extra juice, add water to the pulp and let stand overnight, then strain again.

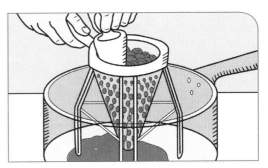

2 **Mash or crush.** Mash juicy berries and grapes to a pulp with a potato masher or in a mortar and pestle. Then strain through a sieve or jelly bag.

3 **Heat and strain.** Cook small pitted fruits, such as cherries, plums, and elderberries, just enough to burst the skins, then strain through a sieve or jelly bag.

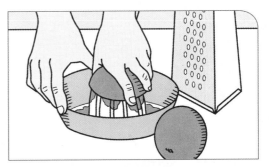

4 **Squeeze.** Extract citrus juices with a juice reamer—mechanical or electric.

5 **Press.** Small-scale cider presses and wine presses are perfect for apples and grapes.

How to Make a Soft Drink

These days, the most popular way to make a soft drink is with a CO_2 charger and soda siphon or antique seltzer bottle. You simply pour juice or regular tap water into the seltzer bottle or soda siphon, which is a stainless-steel canister with a spray device built into the lid. The CO_2 chargers are canisters of pressurized carbon dioxide. The charger fits into the spray head of the bottle or siphon. When you press the trigger or plunger, you will get freshly carbonated seltzer or soda.

The chargers, which are easily available, usually come in boxes of 10, and each charger will carbonate about 1 quart (1 L) of liquid. The seltzer bottles and soda siphons may be made of aluminum, glass, or stainless steel. Bottles with plastic parts are usually not very cost-effective since they do not last very long. The most popular bottles are the stainless-steel ones.

If you don't want to extract your own juice to flavor the soda, you can purchase juice concentrate in black currant, apple, lemon, and blueberry flavors, to name a few. You can also add pieces of fruit and slices of fruit for flavor, including all types of berries, slices of citrus fruit, and bits of peaches or pineapples.

HOMEMADE SOFT DRINKS

Depending on where you live, you may call a carbonated beverage a soft drink, soda, or pop. No matter what you call it, making your own has many advantages, not least of which is knowing exactly what you're drinking. This is also very popular with kids, so get yours into helping you make it and drink it.

WHY MAKE YOUR OWN HOMEMADE SOFT DRINKS?

- No plastic bottles or aluminum cans degrading the environment or in need of recycling

- Made without chemicals, sodium, and artificial ingredients

- No heavy bottles or aluminum cans to lug home

- Saves money

Plums By making your own drinks, you can choose ingredients not normally found in the grocery store. Try a plum soda for a novel soft drink.

Old-Fashioned Fountain Soda

In the old days, when folks couldn't afford a soda fountain setup, they would combine water, concentrated flavoring syrup, and baking soda to make a fizzy drink. There's no excuse to rely on a machine when you can make delicious drinks this way!

2 teaspoons (30 ml) (8 g) sugar
½ teaspoon (2 g) white flour
¼ teaspoon (1.2 g) baking soda

Glass of ice-cold water
2 teaspoons (10 ml) lemon, lime, or orange juice

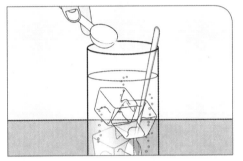

1 Mix the sugar, flour, and baking soda in a glass of ice-cold water until completely dissolved.

2 Then stir in the lemon, lime, or orange juice. Drink while mixture is still frothing. Serves 1.

Soda the Easiest Way

The simplest way to make a soft drink is to combine a fruit juice with store-bought club soda or seltzer. The flavor options are endless, and you could even add a shot of your favorite liquor. Scale up the quantities to make a pitcher to share, and add sugar to taste.

1 cup (250 ml) fresh-squeezed juice
1 cup (250 ml) store-bought seltzer water or club soda

1 Choose your favorite homemade juice.

2 Combine it with a store-bought seltzer water or club soda. Serves 1.

Tomato-Vegetable Juice

Tangy and delicious, this vegetable juice is a perfect afternoon pick-me-up.

10 pounds (4.5 kg) tomatoes, peeled and
    chopped
3 cloves garlic, minced
2 large onions, chopped
2 carrots, cut into ½-inch (1-cm) slices

2 cups (300 g) chopped celery
½ cup (75 g) chopped green pepper
¼ cup (50 g) sugar
½ teaspoon (1 g) pepper
Lemon juice

1 Combine the fruit and vegetables in a soup kettle. Bring to a boil, and simmer for 20 minutes or until vegetables are soft. Cool. Press mixture through a fine sieve.

2 Return the juice to the soup kettle. Add sugar and pepper. Bring to a boil. Add lemon juice to taste. Store in the refrigerator. Makes 7–8 quarts (7–8 L).

Zesty Lemonade

This lemonade is a life saver on a hot day. Enjoy it ice-cold all through the summer.

1 cup (200 g) sugar
1 cup (250 ml) water (for the simple syrup)
1 cup (250 ml) lemon juice (4–6 lemons)
3–4 cups (750 ml–1 L) cold water

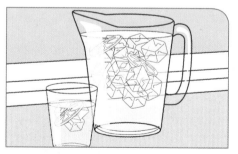

1 Make the syrup by heating the sugar and water in a small saucepan until dissolved. Meanwhile, squeeze the lemon juice into a bowl.

2 In a pitcher, combine the juice and syrup. Add the cold water. Refrigerate 30–40 minutes. Serve with ice. Serves 6.

Berry Refresher

This tantalizing berry drink keeps well in the refrigerator, so you can enjoy it for months.

4 cups (600 g) fresh berries (blackberries are good)
2 cups (500 ml) cider vinegar
2 cups (375 g) granulated sugar
Water for diluting to taste

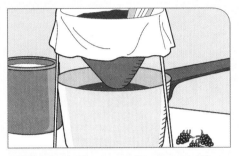

1 Place berries in nonmetal bowl, cover with vinegar, and steep for 3–4 days. Strain through cheesecloth into a pan and stir in sugar. Boil 2–3 minutes, remove from heat, and let cool.

2 Store in a tightly covered jar or pitcher. Will keep for 12 months if stored in the refrigerator. Dilute with water to taste. Makes about 6 cups.

Homemade Orange Soda

Made with fresh juice, this recipe is delicious and packed full of vitamin C.

1½ cups (350 ml) fresh-squeezed orange juice
2 12-ounce cans lemon-lime soft drink, chilled
1–2 oranges, thinly sliced

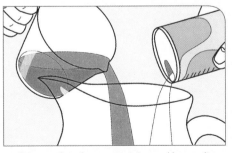

1 Stir together the orange juice and lemon-lime soft drink when ready to serve.

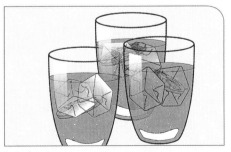

2 Serve over ice in individual glasses with an orange slice. Serves 4.

FLAVORED LIQUORS AND LIQUEURS

Make homemade liquors and liqueurs using crops from your own garden. Not only is the process fairly easy, but the end result is delicious and makes an impressive presentation in the bottle—great for gift-giving.

Homemade Fruit Liqueurs

It is easy to make fruit liqueurs using apricots, black currants, lemons, blueberries, cherries, cranberries, nectarines, peaches, plums, and raspberries.

1 pound (450 g) berries or fruit

3 cups (700 ml) 70-proof vodka (or 1½ cups [350 ml] pure grain alcohol plus 1½ cups [350 ml] water)

1¼ cups (275 g) granulated sugar, plus extra to taste

1 Wash the berries or fruit. Cut fruit into small pieces and remove any pits.

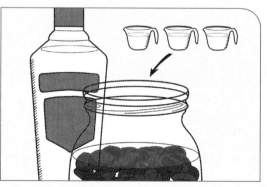

2 Place in a 2-quart (2-L) jar, and add the vodka or grain alcohol and water mixture. Cover and store in a cool, dark place.

3 Stir once a week for 2–4 weeks.

4 Strain and discard the fruit. Transfer the unsweetened liqueur to a glass bottle. Add the granulated sugar. Let age for at least 3 months.

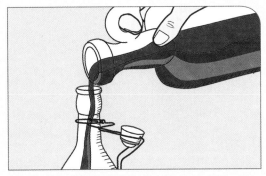

5 Carefully pour into a clean bottle. Add more sugar to taste, if necessary. If your liqueur is too sweet, add a mixture of vodka and water (1:1).

6 The flavor will continue to improve. Most fruit and berry liqueurs should be stored for at least 6 months for maximum flavor, although lemon liqueurs should be stored for only 1 or 2 months.

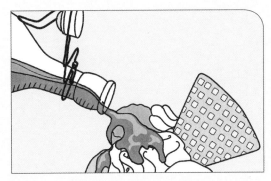

7 Sip after dinner or pour over ice cream for a quick, colorful dessert.

Method: Making Herb-Infused Vodka

This recipe makes a crisp drink perfect for winter evenings and for entertaining friends.

½ cup (75 g) to 2 cups (300 g) of spices or herbs per quart (liter) of vodka

1 Prepare the infusion. Put the flavoring in a large, clean glass jar. Leave small berries whole, but chop most other fruits and vegetables. Slice vanilla pods lengthwise with a knife; bruise fresh herb leaves to release the oil. Add the vodka. Reserve the original bottle and top. Close the jar tightly. Set aside in a cool, dark place.

2 Allow to infuse. Most infusions take 7–10 days; some are ready overnight, and others take up to 3 months. It depends on the potency of the ingredients and how strong you want the flavor. The only way to know whether the infusion is ready is to taste it periodically.

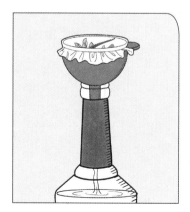

3 When the vodka is to your liking, strain out the solids. Use a funnel lined with cheesecloth or a coffee filter. Transfer the infused vodka back into the original vodka bottle. Store in a cool, dark place.

HOW TO MAKE FLAVORED VODKAS

Flavored vodkas, also called infusions, are popular in cocktails, but why pay extra money when you can make your own and avoid artificial flavorings and ingredients? No special equipment or ingredients are required.

Start with a good-quality vodka—don't spend money on a top-shelf brand, but don't use the cheapest one either. Spices, herbs, and fruit are most frequently used to flavor the vodka: The amount you need depends on how flavorful the ingredients are and how quickly you'd like the infusion to be completed. Most recipes call for ½ cup (75g) to 2 cups (300 g) of fruit per quart (L) of vodka, but smaller quantities of highly flavored ingredients, like chile peppers or ginger, are used.

Herbal Teas Proven restorative cures, aids to weight loss, and generally healthful, real herbal teas are in high demand in health-food stores.

HERBAL TEAS

You can make tea with common kitchen herbs, including basil, fennel, marjoram, thyme, rosemary, and mint. Cloves, ginger, nutmeg, and orange zest often flavor spice teas, and rose petals and lemon verbena are just a couple of the common plant ingredients that make lovely tea. Some of the best boldest-tasting teas are a healthy mixture of flowers, herbs, and weeds.

The Benefits of Herbal Teas

Herbs can sometimes act as great medicines, and they have strong restorative powers. The perfect way to make the most of their abilities is by using them fresh from your garden to make aromatic teas.

Which Herbs to Use

- **Mint** eases stomach and digestive problems, helps relieve headaches, and is relaxing.

- **Borage** aids stress relief, promotes relaxation, and has a calming effect.

- **Fennel** helps bronchitis, digestive problems, and coughs, and it destroys germs. It makes a good after-dinner tea. Use crushed or ground seeds.

- **Lemon balm** will perk you up in the morning, and help relieve bloating, gas, bronchial inflammation, high blood pressure, toothache, earache, and headaches. Lemon balm has antibacterial and antiviral properties. Use the leaves. A good combination is lemon balm and fennel.

- **Thyme** helps ease bronchitis and sinus pain and relieves nose and throat inflammation. It can be used as an antibacterial. Thyme tea also aids digestion.

HOW TO MAKE HERBAL TEAS

Bring water to a boil. Add 2 tablespoons (6 g) herbs to a mug and add the just-boiled water. Cover and let the herbs steep. The amount of time to let the tea infuse depends on the herbs used—it is really a case of trial and error. Some herbs will begin to taste bitter if left too long. Taste the tea intermittently to gauge how long it should be left. Strain the herbs before drinking.

Alternatively, place the herbs in a saucepan of cold water and slowly bring to a boil. As soon as the water reaches the boiling point, take it off the heat, strain, and enjoy.

To make more than one serving, use a teapot. The general rule is that for every cup (250 ml) of water in the pot, add 1 teaspoon (5 ml) of chopped herbs, and then 1 final, extra spoonful. That means for 5 people, the pot gets 6 teaspoons of herbs.

Sweeten your tea to taste; this does not affect its restorative powers. Taste each tea before deciding whether or not to add milk or honey.

Parsley and Thyme
Teas made with these herbs are aromatic and good for easing the symptoms of colds and flu.

WINEMAKING

Making your own wine is part art, part science. The scientist assembles the right ingredients and conditions to allow fermentation to convert sugar into alcohol, but the artist decides how, when, and where to perform each step along the way.

Growing your own grapes is possible in a surprisingly wide range of climates because of new wine-grape varieties. You can make wine from other fruits as well. You can also buy grape juice suitable for winemaking.

Basic Winemaking Equipment

Equipment for winemaking is found at any home-brewing or home-winemaking supply shop or online. Here's what you will need for a 1-gallon (4-L) batch.

GOOD FRUIT FOR WINEMAKING	AMOUNT OF FRUIT NEEDED	AMOUNT OF SUGAR NEEDED
Damson plums	22 lb (10 kg)	14 lb (6.5 kg)
Black currants	9 lb (4 kg)	14 lb (6.5 kg)
Plums	17 lb 6 oz (8 kg)	14 lb (6.5 kg)
Strawberries	11 lb (5 kg)	14 lb (6.5 kg)
Cherries	22 lb (10 kg)	14 lb (6.5 kg)
Raspberries	9 lb (4 kg)	14 lb (6.5 kg)
Sour apples	22 lb (10 kg)	14 lb (6.5 kg)
Pears	17 lb 6 oz (8 kg)	14 lb (6.5 kg)
Elderberries	9 lb (4 kg)	14 lb (6.5 kg)
Blackberries	13 lb 3 oz (6 kg)	14 lb (6.5 kg)

- Large nylon straining bag
- Food-grade pail with lid (2–4 gallon [7.5–15 L] capacity)
- Cheesecloth
- Hydrometer
- Thermometer
- Acid titration kit
- Clear, flexible ½-inch-diameter (1-cm) plastic tubing
- Two 1-gallon (3.75-L) glass jugs
- Two airlocks and stoppers
- Five 750-ml wine bottles
- Corks
- Hand corker

Sanitize, Sanitize, Sanitize

Wash all your equipment thoroughly with hot water, sterilizing what you can by boiling for 10 minutes in a large pot or running through the sterilizing cycle on your dishwasher. It's also wise to use a strong sulfite solution to rinse any equipment that comes in contact with your wine. To make it, add 3 tablespoons (45 ml) of sulfite powder (potassium metabisulfite) or 1 Campden tablet to 1 gallon (4 L) of water and mix well. Sanitizing inhibits airborne wild yeasts from contaminating your wine and makes a big difference in the final flavor of the wine.

Method: Making Red Wine

For your first batch of wine, it is wise to make a small batch as you learn the process and make decisions on how to make wine best suited to your taste. For this first experiment, plan to make 5 bottles of red wine from 18 pounds (8 kg) of ripe red grapes. Red wines always are fermented with the skins and pulp, and the juice is pressed after fermentation is complete. White wines are always pressed before fermentation, so only the grape juice winds up in the fermenting pail. Harvest your grapes once they have reached 22–24 percent sugar (22°–24° Brix).

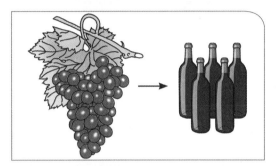

1 Winemaking starts with ripe fruit. The fruit should be clean and free from insects, stems (which will make the wine bitter), and other debris. Mash up some of your fruit and measure the sugar level with a hydrometer.

2 Assemble your ingredients. You will need:

- 18 pounds (5 kg) ripe red grapes
- 1 Campden tablet (or 1 ounce [30 g] of potassium metabisulfite powder)
- Tartaric acid, if necessary
- Granulated white sugar, if necessary
- 1 packet wine yeast (such as Prise de Mousse or Montrachet)

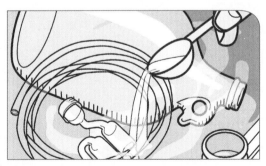

3 Sanitize all your equipment by washing in a weak bleach solution (combine 1 tablespoon [15 ml] household bleach with 1 gallon [4 L] water, then rinse with boiling water.

4 Put the grapes in the nylon straining bag and set the bag in a food-grade pail. Firmly crush the grapes inside the bag, using your hands or a potato masher to make the "must." Crush the Campden tablet (or measure out 1 teaspoon [5 ml] of sulfite crystals) and sprinkle it over the must. Cover the pail with cheesecloth and let it sit for 1 hour.

(continued on page 148)

5 Measure the temperature of the must. It should be 70–75° F (20–25° C). If needed, warm by wrapping the pail with an electric blanket; chill by packing in ice.

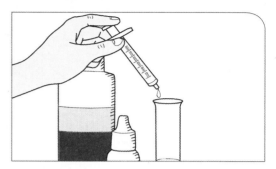

6 For dry reds, the ideal acid level is 65 percent (or 7.5 g/L); for dry whites it is 75 percent (or 7.5g/L). Adjust with tartaric acid as needed.

7 Check the degrees Brix or specific gravity of the must with the hydrometer. It should be around 22° Brix (1.0982 SG). To increase the sugar concentration, make a sugar syrup by combining 1 cup (200 g) sugar and ⅓ cup (80 ml) water. Bring to a boil, stir to dissolve the sugar, and immediately remove from heat. Cool before adding 1 tablespoon (15 ml) at a time, until the desired degrees Brix and specific gravity is reached. To lower the sugar level, dilute the must with cooled, boiled water.

8 Dissolve the yeast in 2 cups (475 ml) warm water and let stand until bubbly, 5–10 minutes. Pour the yeast solution directly on the must inside the nylon bag. Shake the bag a few times to mix in the yeast. Cover the pail with cheesecloth and set it in a warm area. Fermentation should begin within 24 hours (you will see bubbles rising in the must).

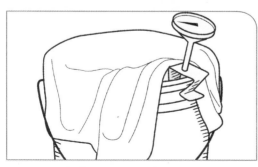

9 Monitor the fermentation and temperature regularly, and mix twice daily. Make sure the skins remain submerged in the juice at all times. The ideal fermentation temperature is 70° F (20° C) for red wines.

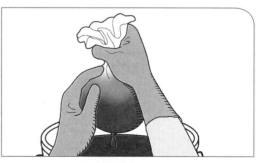

10 Once the must has reached "dryness" (at least 0.5° Brix or 0.998 SG), indicating the sugar has been converted to alcohol, lift the nylon straining bag out of the pail and squeeze any remaining liquid into the pail.

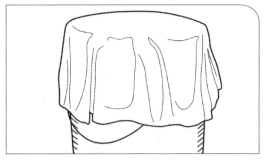

11 Cover the pail loosely and let the wine settle for 24 hours.

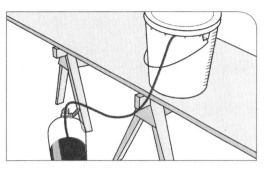

12 The next step is to "rack" the wine, meaning that you will siphon off the fermenting wine away from sediment. To do so, insert a clear ½-inch-diameter (1-cm) plastic hose into the fermenting must and siphon the clear wine into another sanitized jug. This can be a delicate operation, and it's important to go slowly so you don't stir up the sediment. Then top off the clear wine with cooled, boiled water to entirely fill the jug. Fit it with a sanitized stopper and airlock.

13 Leave for 10 days, keeping the jug topped with grape juice or any dry red wine of a similar style. After 10 days, rack the wine into another sanitized 1-gallon (4-L) jug. Top off with dry red wine of a similar style.

14 Leave for 6 months in a cool, dark place.

15 Siphon the clear wine off the sediment and into clean, sanitized bottles. Cork with the hand-corker.

16 Store the bottles in a cool, dark place, and wait at least 6 months before drinking.

BREWING BEER

Ever since home brewing of beers was made legal in the United States in 1978, enthusiasts have been brewing beer in small batches. Many have been so successful, they have taken their beer-brewing skills to the next level—establishing microbreweries for profit. The equipment and ingredients needed for home-scale beer brewing are all available at home-brewing supply stores.

·BEER·

He was a wise man who invented beer.

—Plato

Basic Equipment for Brewing Beer

- Stockpot—should hold at least 2 gallons (7.5 L)
- Clear, flexible ½-inch-diameter (1-cm) plastic tubing, at least 5 feet (1.5 m) long
- 7-gallon (28-L) glass carboy (for fermenting the beer)
- Airlock and stopper (releases carbon dioxide from the fermenter without letting air in)
- Bottles
- Bottle caps and capper
- Food-grade bucket

Ingredients

As a beginner, consider buying a preassembled beer kit that contains all the necessary ingredients for brewing one batch of beer. Otherwise, you will need malt extract, corn sugar, hops, and yeast.

Water If the tap water at your house tastes good to you, it is fine to use for beer brewing; otherwise use bottled or distilled water. If you do use tap water, boil it first to evaporate the chlorine and other chemicals that may interfere with the brewing process. Let the water cool before using.

Malted Barley Extract This provides the sugar to keep the yeast alive.

Hops These flowers lend the bitter flavor to beer that balances out sweetness. Hops also inhibit spoilage and help keep the "head" (the frothy top when a beer is poured) around longer.

Yeast Beer yeast is cultivated especially for use in brewing; it is not the same as baking yeast. There are two broad categories of beer yeast: ale and lager. Ale yeasts are top-fermenting, which means they tend to hang out at the top of the carboy while fermenting and rest at the bottom after the majority of fermenting has occurred. Ale yeasts will not actively ferment below 50° F (10° C). Lager yeasts are bottom-fermenters and are best used at a temperature ranging from 32°–55° F (0°–12° C).

Sanitize, Sanitize, Sanitize

Wash all your equipment thoroughly with hot water. Then sanitize all your materials with household bleach or with an iodine solution that can be bought at your local home-brew store. (To make a bleach disinfecting solution, combine 1 tablespoon [15 ml] bleach and 1 gallon [4 L] water.) Be sure to rinse the equipment well with boiling water before using it. Sanitizing inhibits airborne wild yeasts from contaminating your beer and makes a big difference in the final flavor of the beer.

Method: Making Homemade Beer

Beer brewing starts with making a "wort," a soupy mixture of malt and sugar. Then the wort is combined with yeast and allowed to ferment. A second fermentation takes place in the bottle. For your first experiment, make a simple ale, as described below.

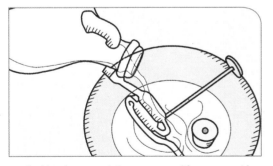

1 Sanitize the pot, stirring spoon, and fermenter with the sanitizing solution. Rinse everything in boiling water.

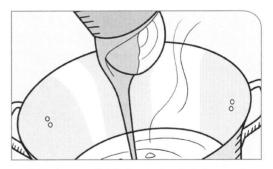

2 Bring 6 quarts (5.5 L) of water to a boil. Remove from the heat and stir in the malt syrup until it dissolves. Return the pot to the heat and bring the mixture to a boil. Boil for 50 minutes, stirring frequently. Reduce the heat if the mixture threatens to boil over.

(continued on page 152)

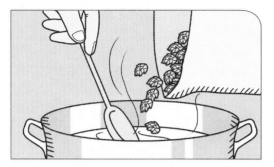

3 Stir in the hop pellets. The hops will create a foam on the top of the liquid. To avoid having the hops boil up over the top of the pot, lower the heat or spray the foam down with a water bottle. Let the hops cook for 10–20 minutes.

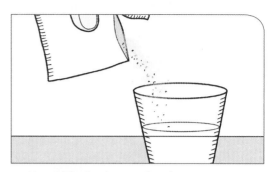

4 Meanwhile, dissolve 1 packet of yeast in 1 cup (250 ml) very warm water (90° F/32° C); stir and cover for 10 minutes. If the yeast does not begin to bubble, discard the yeast solution and try again with the second yeast packet. Also prepare an ice-cold water bath in either a large sink or tub to quickly cool the wort.

5 Quickly cool the wort by placing it in the ice bath and stirring constantly until the wort reaches 80° F (25° C).

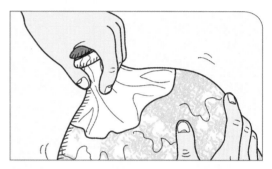

6 Pour 3 gallons (11 L) cool water into your sanitized carboy. Add the wort and yeast. Cover the carboy's mouth with plastic wrap and cap it with a lid. Holding your hand tightly over the lid, shake the carboy to distribute the yeast. Remove the plastic wrap, wipe off any wort around the carboy's mouth, and secure the top with the airlock (with a little water added into its top).

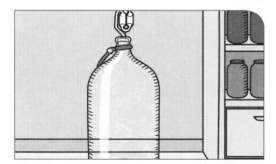

7 Store the carboy in a cool spot for about 2 weeks. Fermentation will begin within 24 hours. A clear sign of fermentation is the production of foam and air bubbles in the fermentation lock.

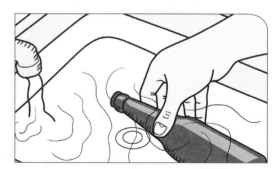

8 Sanitize all of your bottles by soaking them in the sanitizing solution (make sure to hold them under the solution so the water gets inside of the bottles) for 1 hour. Rinse the bottles with boiling water. Also sanitize a small cooking pot, bottling bucket, and siphon. Follow the instructions that came with the bottle caps to sanitize them. Let everything air-dry.

9 Combine ¾ cup (175 ml) liquid corn syrup (or 4 ounces/120 g dry corn sugar) and 1 cup (250 ml) water in the pot. Bring to a boil and boil for 10 minutes. Pour into the bottling bucket. Place the carboy on a kitchen counter and the bottling bucket on the floor below it.

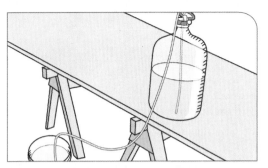

10 Place one end of the sanitized siphon into the carboy and the other end into a jar; once the beer has begun flowing through the siphon, transfer its end to the bottling bucket. Monitor the speed that the beer transfers into the bottling bucket by pinching and releasing the siphon with your fingers (or a clamp). Once all the beer has been siphoned into the bucket, cover it and wait 30 minutes for the sediment to settle at the bottom of the bucket.

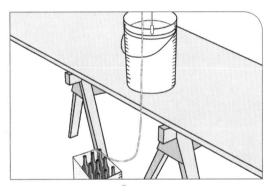

11 Place the bottling bucket on the counter, attach the siphon, and run the other end of the siphon into a bottle. Fill each bottle with beer to ¾ inch (2 cm) from the top of the bottle. Cap each bottle with the bottle-capper.

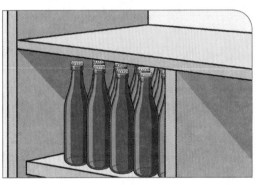

12 Age the bottles at room temperature for at least 2 weeks, or up to 2 months.

SIGNATURE BREWING

Try different ingredients in your beer— maybe add spices or syrups. There are no hard-and-fast rules. Some of the greatest beers in history are the ones made by people who broke the rules.

MAKING CIDER AND VINEGAR

Making cider (and wine) has long been associated with making vinegar. In apple-growing regions, cider vinegar is made from cider, whereas in grape-growing regions, wine vinegar is made from wine. In each case, a "mother," which is a mass of bacteria and other sediments, is added to the cider or wine and allowed to do its work. The "mother" turns the wine or cider into vinegar, or acetic acid.

Cider

Cider is made by pressing fresh apples to extract all the juice. There are plenty of small-scale cider presses available that you can purchase online if making cider is something you plan to do on a yearly basis. But you can make a batch in your kitchen just to see if this is something you want to attempt on a regular basis.

First gather your apples. Cider tastes best when a variety of apple types are used, blending both tart flavors and sweet. Wash the apples thoroughly, cutting out any bruises or damaged parts. Quarter the apples, leaving the skins on them for color. Purée the apple quarters completely in a food processor or blender. Squeeze the puréed apple through a cheesecloth, extracting all the juice possible. The cider will be cloudy (compared to clear bottled apple juice). Store the cider in a sealed container in the refrigerator, or freeze for extended storage.

Vinegar

Making vinegar is so easy that it often happens by accident—a bottle of wine or cider comes in contact with wild yeasts in the air and turns to vinegar. But you can control the process and make vinegar that you will be happy to use in salad dressings and other recipes. (Do not use homemade vinegar to make pickles; it may not be acidic enough to safely preserve the vegetables.)

Vinegar can be made from almost anything that contains sugar or starch, but the process is easiest when you start with apple cider. After you get the hang of making apple cider vinegar, you may want to explore making other types, such as wine vinegar. You will need a large glass jar (do not use plastic or metal). Fill it with freshly made cider. Add some unpasturized, unfiltered vinegar, available at most health-food stores. Do not use mass-marketed supermarket vinegars; they have been pasteurized and will not contain the necessary bacteria culture. Combine the fresh cider and unpasteurized vinegar (see recipe on page 155). Leave it in a warm, dark place for 4 to 6 months. Light will slow the vinegar production or even kill your culture. The precise temperature is not critical; room temperature is ideal to keep the rate of fermentation neither too fast or too slow.

After 4 months, begin checking the vinegar until it is as strong as you like it, or until it seems to be losing strength. Bottle it in small bottles and leave for at least six months before using. The aging will make the flavor smoother.

Homemade Sparkling Cider

Your own homemade cider is fruity and refreshing in summer but can be spicy and warming in winter. Add your favorite spices for a distictive flavor.

5 gallons (19 L) fresh-pressed apple juice
5 cups (950 g) sugar
1.75 ounce package (125 ml) liquid lager brewer's yeast (available from beer-brewing supply stores)

1 Transfer the juice and sugar into a sanitized stainless-steel container. Dissolve the sugar, and add the lager yeast and a fermentation lock. The mixture will bubble, releasing carbon dioxide as the yeast converts the sugars into alcohol.

2 Allow the cider to ferment for at least 2 months before transferring it into bottles, a keg, or any container you prefer.

Homemade Cider Vinegar

With this recipe, you can add a personal splash of flavor to meals, making your own delicious salad dressing and vinaigrettes with homemade ingredients.

1 quart (1 L) unfiltered, unpasteurized vinegar
1 quart (1 L) fresh unfiltered, unpasteurized cider

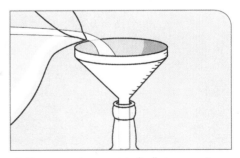

1 Pour the unpasteurized, unfiltered vinegar into the pitcher. Add the apple juice, mix, and place in a warm, dark place for 4–6 months.

2 Taste your vinegar periodically to assess its taste, then transfer into bottles.

THE
SUSTAINABLE
HOME

Part of growing your own produce and learning how to prepare and preserve your crop is making your household more sustainable, saving money, helping the environment, and maintaining a culinary peace of mind. As well as growing fresh garden fruits and vegetables, there are other ways to live more independently.

This chapter includes advice on raising chickens in your backyard, beekeeping, forming community gardens, and making your own yogurt and cheese. Learn the basics of equipment and techniques to expand your self-sufficiency skills. The home-grown eggs, honey, and homemade dairy products will taste superb, and you can rest easy knowing there are no additives or adverse effects on the environment. You can even turn self-sufficiency into a small business, supplying all-natural products to friends and neighbors. All the techniques included in this chapter are easy to begin, so you can be on your way to sustainability in no time.

ON THE WAY TO SELF-SUFFICIENCY

Growing your own food ensures that you're ingesting fewer pesticides and growth hormones. You'll save money and have home-raised food and beverages to enjoy all year long.

RAISING CHICKENS

If you want a sustainable household, raising chickens can be a fun and exciting adventure. They provide fresh eggs and meat for a fraction of what you pay at the store. You know exactly what they have been fed and can assure their quality. Chickens also are great for gardeners, because they eat weeds and pests and provide fertilizer in the form of manure.

•CHICKENS•

The key to everything is patience. You get the chicken by hatching the egg, not by smashing it.

—Arnold H. Glasgow

Getting Started

Chickens are generally classed in four categories: meat birds, egg layers, dual-purpose, and novelty breeds (for show). Decide what you want from your birds, and then get advice from your local cooperative extension agent, feed store, or farmers to determine which breeds will work best in your area.

How big a flock would you like? Once hens start laying (at about 5 months), they generally give one egg per day throughout their laying period (14–16 months). For a family of four, 6–10 hens will provide enough eggs.

You can start your flock with fertilized eggs (this requires an incubator), day-old chicks, or young pullets. Be sure you buy from reputable hatcheries. Generally chicks are shipped at any time of the year except winter. If you live where the winters are cold, time the arrival of the chicks for no earlier than April 1.

Chick Housing Young chicks require warmth and protection. The housing can be as simple as a sturdy, 18-inch-tall (45-cm) cardboard box. Line the bottom of the box with newspaper and then add at least

4 inches (10 cm) of fresh wood shavings, cane fiber, ground corncobs, peanut hulls, or rice hulls. Clean the litter as often as needed.

Each chick needs 1 square foot (30 sq cm) of "walking space" until they are about 8 weeks old. At that point, they need at least 2 square feet (45 sq cm) of floor space or be allowed to range outside during the day.

The temperature within the box should be kept at 90°–100° F (35° C) for the first week. Infrared lamps work best, but a 100-watt bulb may also be used. Hang the lamp about 18 inches (45 cm) above the litter. Raise the bulb 2 inches (5 cm) per week to a maximum height of 24 inches (60 cm). If the chicks are staying huddled under the light, the box is too cold. Your chickens will be up and walking around their box during the day and sleeping under the light at night.

Care and Feeding of Chicks Give your chicks access to feed (one pie plate for every 30 chicks) and water from a chick waterer at all times for the first 7 days. Afterward, one tube-type feeder and one 2-gallon (7.5-L) waterer are needed. Keep the feeders and waterers clean and adjusted so that the trough position is level with the back height of the birds.

Provide the chicks with starter feed until they are 6 weeks old. Then you can mix the starter with a "developer" feed until they are 20 weeks old. At this time you can switch over to a "layer" feed. Treats for the chickens can include vegetables, bread, bugs, and chicken scratch (cracked corn, millet, and wheat).

Hen Housing

Any well-ventilated structure that protects the chickens from predators, cold, and rain can be used as a chicken coop. It needs to provide 3–4 square feet (1 sq m) per chicken. Be sure to cover the floor with litter; pine shavings work well. The structure must also protect feeders and be suitable for nests and a roost. Tube feeders and an automatic waterer are recommended.

Nests Provide one nest per four layers. Nest boxes should be about 12–14 inches square (30–35 sq cm). Build the nest boxes 24 inches (60 cm) above the litter. Place nesting material, such as shavings or hay, in the nests and replace it frequently to keep the eggs clean.

Roosts Laying hens require roosts; allow at least 8 inches (20 cm) of space per bird. Locate the poles 14 inches (35 cm) apart and 18–36 inches (45–90 cm) above the litter. Be sure to screen the dropping pit beneath the roost to keep the birds out and to minimize internal parasite problems. Keep the manure dry to prevent fly problems.

Eggs

Collect eggs twice daily and allow them to cool rapidly by placing a damp cloth over the top. Store eggs in a cool, dark place in wooden or cardboard boxes.

BEEKEEPING

When it comes to beekeeping, a small investment in equipment can result in a huge return in the form of honey and beeswax, and the bees do most of the work for you. Bees will travel far to collect nectar and pollen, so they do not even need flowering plants close by. Before getting started, familiarize yourself with local "nuisance laws," which may restrict your beekeeping to a certain number of hives or require a certain height of fencing.

Equipment

Set up your colony in the spring with one or two hives and bees from a reputable source. Before ordering bees, check with local beekeepers about the preferred types of honeybees (Italian, Carniolan, and Caucasian are the most popular) for your region.

Beehives These are made up of four-sided, bottomless boxes called supers. Each hive has a bottom board and metal-sheathed cover. Frames, which are filled with a wax sheet stamped with a honeycomb pattern, are set in the hives and provide a foundation upon which the bees build their combs. The hives also include wire or plastic queen excluders, which allow worker bees to pass through while preventing the passage of the queen.

Entrance Reducers Also called cleats, these wooden or plastic blocks partially close entrances to prevent robbing or mice from entering the hive

Bee Feeders Typically gallon (4-L) jars with small holes in the cap that fit into a hole drilled into the hive cover

Smoker This is for calming, not punishing, your bees. You will get used to using it to maintain harmony within your hive

Uncapping Knife Electrically heated knife to cut the caps off honeycombs

Beekeeping Clothing White coveralls, elbow-length gloves, veil, and hat

Locating the Hive

Place the hives near a windbreak, but be sure it is in a sunny spot for warmth. If the entrance receives the morning sun, the bees will be more productive, becoming active early in the day. Keep the hive off the ground on concrete blocks or a

Safety Your smoker will help keep the bees calm and under control to avoid unnecessary injuries or swarms.

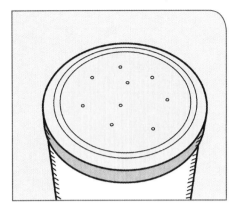

Bee Feeder
Keep your bees happy and healthy using the right bee feeder for your type of honeybees.

·HONEY·

The only reason for being a bee that I know of is making honey... and the only reason for making honey is so I can eat it.

— Winnie the Pooh in A. A. Milne's *The House at Pooh Corner*

a wooden pallet, which is gently sloping forward to allow rain and snow to drain. If neighbors live nearby, put the entrance of the hive facing a high fence to force the bees to fly in a high flight pattern.

Establishing Your Apiary

The bees will arrive from your supplier in a wooden box with screened sides, containing about 12,000 live adult workers (approximately 3 pounds/1.5 kg), one newly mated queen bee, and an inverted can of sugar water. There may be as much as an inch (2 cm) of dead bees in the bottom of the box—see pages 162–3 for what to do with live ones.

Simple hive tool used for prying, scraping, and basic hive repair.

Frame lifter and scraper used to pry the edges of the frame bars when removing them, removing nails, and as a hammer.

Stainless-steel hive tool needed for prying, scraping, and simple hive repair. Includes a nail-pulling hole.

Brushes and Tools You will need various sizes of tools for opening the hive, separating the combs, scraping the hive parts, and working the nails at the time of hive inspection.

Bee brush

Method: How to Set Up Beekeeping

Time the arrival of your bees for the spring, when the temperatures generally exceed 57° F. Have the hives and all the equipment ready for the arrival of the bees.

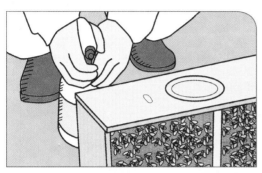

1 Place the box on its side in a cool, dark spot. Make a gallon (4 L) of sugar water (1 part granulated or powdered sugar to 1 part water) and put it in a spray bottle. Spray the bees with sugar syrup. Repeat periodically until the bees are full and stop eating.

2 Gather together a hive tool, a smoker, and a spray bottle filled with sugar syrup. Wear full protective clothing.

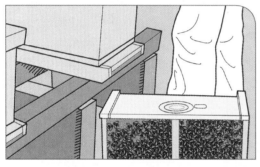

3 Feed the bees again with sugar syrup, and carry the box to the hives. Place the box on the ground in a shaded area.

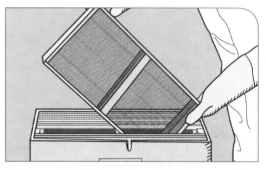

4 Remove three or four frames from the center of the brood chamber to create a space in the hive for the bees. Spray the bees again with sugar syrup.

5 With the hive tool, remove the panel from the box of bees. Gently remove the feeder and queen cage from the hole in the top of the box. Shake bees from the outside of the queen cage and inspect the queen to ensure that she is still alive and healthy. Place the queen cage in the shade. Replace the panel over the hole to prevent bees from escaping. (If the queen is dead, immediately order a new queen and have it shipped overnight. Follow instructions on package for introducing this "stranger" to the hive.)

6 Firmly knock the box on the ground once to make the bees drop to the bottom. Remove the cover and quickly invert the box over the hive body. Firmly and vigorously shake the bees into the space in the hive. Prop the box in front of the entrance of the hive so that any remaining bees can crawl into the hive. Return the frames to the hive.

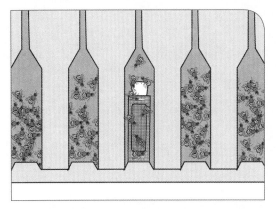

7 To install the queen, remove the plastic cap from the long side of the queen cage with the white sugar candy. Place the queen cage candy-side up between two center frames of the hive. The bees will eat the candy and release the queen in a day or two.

8 Feed the new colony with sugar syrup. Replace the inner cover and lid.

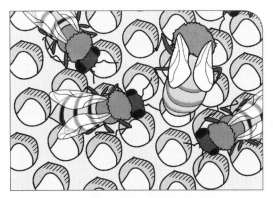

9 Inspect the colony in 5 days to ensure that the queen is alive and has been released. Inspect the colony again after another 5 days to verify that the queen has begun laying eggs (they look like small grains of rice standing up in the center of cells). If necessary, add more sugar syrup. Keep them well supplied until there is a sufficient supply of honey stored in the colony.

10 To prevent the overcrowding that leads to swarming, add additional supers (see page 160) when half of the frames in the first hive body are fully drawn out.

Method: How to Harvest Your Honey

Generally you cannot harvest honey until after the second summer, when a well-established hive will yield 30–60 pounds (15 to 30 kg) of honey each year. You need to leave a full super or second hive body and at least 30 pounds (15 kg) of honey in the brood nest. This will amount to a total of 70 pounds (35 kg) of honey for the bees' consumption. Harvest the honey from your hive when the bees have capped at least three-quarters of the cells in the frames.

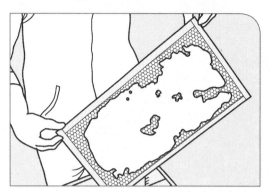

1 Remove the frames from the hive one at a time and inspect them to be sure they are sufficiently filled and sealed. Make sure there is no brood on the frame. There will be bees on the frame; make sure you do not have the queen. If you do see the queen, very gently brush her back into the hive between frames. Then carefully and gently brush the bees back into the hive, using a bee brush, soft flowers, or grass. Put the honey frame (without any bees) in an empty box and cover. Repeat until you have removed enough frames.

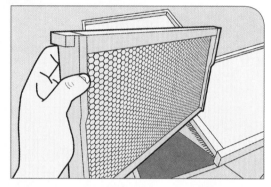

2 If you have some empty frames, put them in the box now. If not, return empty honey frames as soon as you've extracted them. If you leave the bees with empty space for more than a few days, they will start to fill it with wax comb. This will become a mess. It will be hard to return the frames because the space will be full of new comb.

3 Put the lid back on your hive. Take the box frames away to extract your honey.

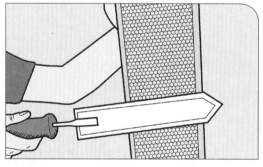

4 Remove the "cappings," the layer of wax from the top of the cells.

5 Place the uncapped frames of comb and honey into an extractor. Spin the frames. Return the emptied combs to the hive for reuse. Enjoy the honey!

Honey Harvest You can add the delicious honey crop from your hive to homemade yogurt for a breakfast treat.

MAKING YOGURT

Yogurt is easy to make, is very economical, and avoids the problem of buying and recycling dozens of plastic containers each week. An added advantage: It can be made with healthful live cultures and without using any artificial ingredients.

Ingredients

All you need to make yogurt is milk and a small amount of cultured plain yogurt. The milk can be whole or lowfat. If you use lowfat milk, you can enrich it with nonfat dry milk, and it won't taste like lowfat yogurt.

Equipment

Making yogurt requires a warm environment. You can provide that warm environment with an electric yogurt maker or something improvised, such as a picnic cooler lined with a heating pad. Or, instead of the heating pad, use large bottles filled with hot water as a heat source. Or you can wrap your containers in blankets and place them in a warm spot (on a shelf above a woodstove or on a radiator, for example).

You will also need two or three glass quart (L) containers (canning jars work very well), a pot, and a kitchen thermometer.

Method: How to Make Yogurt

Despite the proliferation of electric yogurt makers on the market, everything you need to make yogurt is probably already in your kitchen.

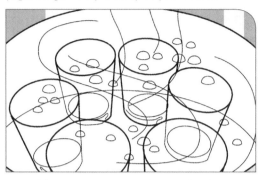

1 **Sterilize the containers.** Submerge the glass containers in a large pot of water and boil for 10 minutes. Or use the sterilizing cycle on your dishwasher.

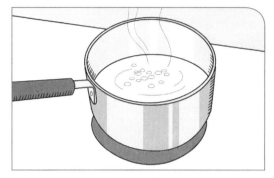

2 **Scald the milk.** Heat the milk to 170°–180° F (around 80° C) to kill any bacteria. Let cool to lukewarm, 105°–110° F (40°–45° C).

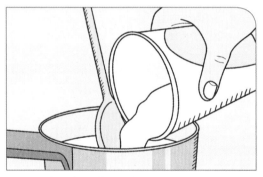

3 **Inoculate the milk.** Stir the plain yogurt starter until liquid. Stir into the milk. Pour the mixture into the containers.

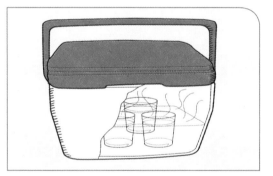

4 **Incubate.** Load the yogurt containers along with the heat source into a cooler. Close the cooler and keep closed to keep the ambient temperature steady. Fermentation takes 4–8 hours (about 6 is ideal). If you are using hot water as a heat source, renew the hot water every 2 hours. Also avoid bumping the cooler; the yogurt needs stillness to firm up.

5 **Check for doneness.** After 4–8 hours (or a bit longer, if the temperature in your cooler is below 100° F/40° C), the yogurt should be firm. Test by gently turning it to see if it keeps its shape. There will be some slightly milky liquid on the top. This is whey. You can either pour it off or just mix it into the yogurt when you eat it.

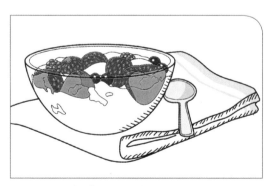

6 **Cover and refrigerate.** The yogurt will last about 2 weeks. Flavor yogurt with honey, maple syrup, sugar, jam, or fruit, if you wish.

MAKING CHEESE

Cheese is one of the oldest foods known to man. It dates back to the earliest domestication of animals, which happened about 9000 B.C. In this context it is easy to see how cheese making can be a highly developed art, which evolved over centuries. But it can also be a simple process, requiring no special equipment or ingredients.

Artisan cheese makers will spend a lifetime perfecting their craft and their recipes. Successful cheese making is not difficult, but it does require time and attention to details.

Ingredients

Milk Cheese can be made from raw or pasteurized cow, goat, or sheep milk. Avoid ultra-pasteurized milk. In general, 1 gallon (4 L) of milk will make 2 pounds (900 g) of soft cheese or 1 pound (450 g) of hard cheese.

Starter Cultures The starter is a bacterial culture that "ripens" the cheese by consuming the lactose in the milk, producing lactic acid, which helps the rennet coagulate the milk. These bacterial cultures give cheese its distinctive flavor. The culture can be buttermilk, which contains an active bacterial culture, or a commercial cheese culture (available online), sometimes called a direct-set starter.

Rennet is an enzyme that acts on protein and causes it to coagulate. It comes in liquid, tablet, and powdered forms and is available online.

Cheese Salt Necessary for both flavor and texture, cheese salt is available online from cheese-making supply houses. You may also substitute coarse kosher salt.

Equipment

Most of the equipment you need to make soft cheeses is probably already in your kitchen, including a large stainless-steel or enamel-lined pot with a cover, a thermometer, and cheesecloth. Some recipes also require a long-bladed stainless-steel carving knife (to cut the curds) and a ladle or large spoon. When you are ready to venture into making semisoft or hard cheeses, you will need additional equipment:

- Thermometer with a temperature range of 0°–212° F (18°–100° C)

- Draining basket or cheese form

- Cheese press

- Cheese wax and a waxing brush (for aged cheese)

Homemade Cheese One of the most beloved foods on Earth, cheese is an easy and popular choice to make for family and friends.

Method: How to Make Cheese

Soft cheeses are much easier to make than hard cheeses and require less equipment, so if you are a beginning cheese maker, this is a good place to start.

1 Heat the milk to 86° F (30° C).

2 Add the starter.

3 Add rennet tablet, powder, or liquid.

4 Set the curd.

5 Cut the curd.

6 Cook the curd.

7 Drain and salt the curd.

8 Mold and press the cheese.

Additionally, the cheese may be aged—protected within a wax coating or allowed to develop a natural rind. Aging cheese successfully requires advanced skills. It is wise to become familiar first with the cheese-making process by starting with something simple, such as making ricotta cheese.

Method: Making Whole-Milk Ricotta Cheese

Before investing in specialized ingredients and equipment, make a simple farmhouse cheese to see if you enjoy the process and the product. Ricotta made from whole milk is extremely easy to make. It does not require a starter culture or rennet. Instead citric acid is added to the milk to cause it to form curds. Citric acid is used to acidify home-canned tomatoes and can be found where canning supplies are sold.

Traditionally ricotta cheese is made from the whey left over from making sheep-milk cheese. But it can be made with whole milk instead. Use this ricotta as you would use store-bought ricotta—in lasagna, as a filling for cannoli, or in cheesecake. The cheese should keep for 1–2 weeks in a covered container in the refrigerator.

1 Combine 1 gallon (4 L) whole milk, 1 teaspoon (5 ml) citric acid, and 1 teaspoon (5 ml) cheese salt in a large stainless-steel pot.

2 Heat the mixture to 185°–195° F (85°–90° C), stirring often to prevent scorching, until curds form and separate from the whey (the whey should not be milky).

3 Remove from the heat and allow to sit undisturbed for 10 minutes. Meanwhile, line a colander with cheesecloth.

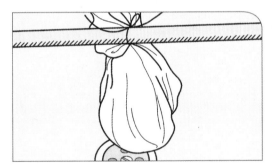

4 Ladle the curds into the cheesecloth. Gather the corners of the cheesecloth together and tie a knot. Hang the bag over the sink and allow to drain for 20–30 minutes, until the cheese has reached a desired consistency.

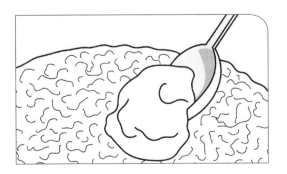

5 For a creamier consistency, stir in 1–2 tablespoons (15–25 ml) heavy cream. Transfer to a container and refrigerate.

EATING LOCALLY NO MATTER WHERE YOU LIVE

One of the most compelling reasons to eat locally is that everything you grow yourself or buy from a farmer at a farmstand or farmers' market most likely has been harvested within the past 24 hours. The produce is ripe, fresh, and full of flavor—unlike supermarket food, which may have been harvested weeks or months before and was bred to withstand long-distance shipping.

Finding Local Foods

It has never been easier to find local suppliers for all of your food needs. Just type "local food" into your favorite Internet search engine, and you will see listings of websites that connect farmers and consumers. It is that simple.

One of the best ways to ensure a steady supply of locally grown foods is to join a CSA (community-supported agriculture). In exchange for a sum of money paid to the farmer at the beginning of the growing season, members get a weekly delivery of vegetables. By paying the farmer up front for his or her crops, you share the risks. So if a flood or hailstorm wipes out one crop, the farmer doesn't lose his shirt. As it turns out, CSA farms are generally diversified farms, and if one crop fails, another one will probably take its place. CSA members are more likely to find that they are getting more vegetables, rather than fewer, than they expected. Some CSA memberships include meat, dairy products, eggs, fruits, flowers, herbs, and other farm products. Many offer social advantages, such as potluck gatherings and opportunities to volunteer at the farm. Many offer opportunities to harvest bumper crops, for those who wish to preserve excess produce. It is good to shop around for the CSA that best meets your needs. The easiest way to locate one near you is to look online.

Locally harvested foods are also found in "whole food" stores and "natural food" stores, as well as food co-ops. Farmers' markets are springing up across the country, and many are including winter markets for year-round access to fresh, locally harvested foods. Some of these local foods, such as Jerusalem artichokes, may be unfamiliar. This is a good thing, underscoring the idea that eating locally is not at all limiting.

Small diversified farms often raise animals as well as vegetables. The animals are a valuable part of the farm ecosystem, providing the farmer with manure to enrich the soil on which the vegetables grow. And vegetable trimmings and seconds that aren't good enough for retail sales can supplement the animal feed. When you shop at a farmers' market, you have a chance to develop a relationship with the farmers, which can often lead to opportunities to buy fresh meat.

Local Foods You can save money and help the environment by shopping for local produce.

Community Gardens

Even if you don't have land, a backyard, or a balcony to hold potted plants, you may be able to raise vegetables through a local community garden organization. Community gardens vary tremendously. They can be found in urban, suburban, and rural areas, as part of schools, hospitals, neighborhoods, and industrial parks, or on vacant city lots. They may be dedicated to growing flowers, vegetables, or fruit.

Generally there is a sponsoring organization and rules for joining the community garden. Some have membership fees, while others require work commitments. Often the sponsoring organization has tilled and improved the soil with compost and other organic materials. Some offer individual plots; some have just one communal garden. Sometimes water is available, sometimes tools. There is no single way to organize a community garden and no single way to keep it running.

But as more people become interested in growing their own food and developing a sustainable local food system, more community gardens are springing up. Browse "community gardens" on your favorite Internet search engine to find a community garden near you.

Eating with the Seasons

When you eat locally, you eat what's in season. Juicy, sweet peaches become the taste of summer; crisp apples, the taste of fall. Winter comfort foods, such as beef stew made with root vegetables, make sense. And your palate will come alive with the first greens of spring.

Seasonal Produce
If you're not harvesting your own crop, buying seasonal fruits and vegetables ensures their freshness.

WATER CONSERVATION

Water conservation makes sense no matter where you live. Even if rainfall is abundant, water conservation can help you save money on your utility bill and prevent water pollution. It may also extend the life of your septic system. Here are some tips to help you conserve water in your home and yard.

- Use your water meter to check for hidden water leaks. Read the house water meter before and after a 2-hour period during which no water is used. If the meter does not read exactly the same, there is a leak. Find it and repair it.

- Reduce the flow of water in your toilet. You can buy an inexpensive float booster or make your own by putting 1–2 inches (3–5 cm) of sand or pebbles inside each of two plastic bottles to weigh them down. Fill the bottles with water, screw the lids on, and put them in your toilet tank, safely away from the operating mechanisms. Be sure at least 3 gallons (11 L) of water remain in the tank so it will flush properly. For new installations, consider buying "low-flush" toilets, which use 1–2 gallons (6 L) per flush instead of the usual 3–5 gallons (12–20 L).

- Insulate your water pipes. Use pre-slit foam pipe insulation to get hot water faster while avoiding wasting water.

- Install water-saving showerheads and low-flow faucet aerators.

- Replace your kitchen sink garbage disposal unit with a compost bucket and outdoor compost pile.

- Water your lawn and garden only when they need it. When watering the lawn, do it long enough for the moisture to soak down to the roots, where it will do the most good.

- Water during the early parts of the day. Avoid watering when it's windy.

- Add organic matter to your soil to increase water retention.

- Plant drought-resistant shrubs and plants.

RESOURCES

Listed below are associations that can provide additional information as well as suppliers of seeds, equipment, and tools. All of these companies have websites. If you don't have a computer at home, you can visit a local library and seek the help of staff.

In the United States

BEEKEEPING

Betterbee, Inc.
Beekeeping and candle-making supplies
8 Meader Road
Greenwich, NY 12834
(800) 632-3379
www.betterbee.com

Brushy Mountain Bee Farm
Beekeeping, candle-making, wine-making supplies
610 Bethany Church Road
Moravian Falls, NC 28654
(336) 921-3640
www.brushymountainbeefarm.com

Dadant and Sons, Inc.
Beekeeping supplies, woodenware, extracting equipment
51 S. 2nd St.
Hamilton, IL 62341
(800) 637-7468
www.dadant.com

Mann Lake Supply
Beekeeping supplies and woodenware
501 First St.
S. Hackensack, MN 56452
(800) 880-7694
www.mannlakeltd.com

Maxant Industries
Honey-processing equipment
P.O. Box 454
Ayer, MA 01432
(978) 772-0576
www.maxantindustries.com

Walter T. Kelly Co., Inc.
Queens, packages, woodenware
P.O. Box 240
Clarkson, KY 42726-0240
(800) 233-2899
www.kelleybees.com

BEER AND WINE

Beer and Wine Hobby
Beer- and wine-making supplies
155 New Boston Street, Unit T
Woburn, MA 01801
(781) 933-8818
www.beer-wine.com

The Home Wine, Beer, and Cheesemaking Shop
Supplies and helpful information for hobbyists
22836 Ventura Boulevard
Woodland Hills, CA 91364
(818) 884-8586
www.homebeerwinecheese.com

CHEESEMAKING

New England Cheesemaking Supply Company
Cheesemaking supplies and recipes
P.O. Box 85
Ashfield, MA 01330
(413) 628-3808
www.cheesemaking.com

GARDENING

Fedco Seeds
Provider of cold-hardy varieties and gardening supplies
P.O. Box 520
Waterville, ME 04903
(207) 873-7333
www.fedcoseeds.com

Johnny's Seeds
Provider of seeds and gardening supplies
955 Benton Avenue
Winslow, ME 04901
(877) 564-6697
www.johnnyseeds.com

National Gardening Association
Information on home, school, and community gardening
1100 Dorset Street
South Burlington, VT 05403
(802) 863-5251
www.garden.org

GENERAL INFORMATION

Cooperative State Research, Education, and Extension Service
A good place to start when embarking on any homesteading type activity
1400 Independence Avenue, Stop 2201
Washington, D.C. 20250-2201
(202) 720-4423
www.csrees.usda.gov/extension/

National Sustainable Agriculture Information Service
Latest news in sustainable agriculture and organic farming
P.O. Box 3657
Fayetteville, AR 72702
www.attra.org

U.S. Department of Agriculture
Publications on a wide range of topics, especially gardening and food preservation
1400 Independence Avenue
Washington, D.C. 20250
(202) 720-2791
www.usda.gov

PRESERVING

All Season Homestead Helpers
Equipment for gardeners, home
canners, and do-it-yourselfers
Routes 15 and 108
Jeffersonville, VT 05464
(800) 649-9147
www.homesteadhelpers.com

Jarden Home Brands
Ball and Kerr lines of canning
products, recipes, preserving guides,
how-to information
14611 West Commerce Road
P.O. Box 529
Daleville, IN 47334
(800) 240-3340
www.freshpreserving.com

Kitchen Krafts
Supplies for home canning, home
baking, and candymaking
P.O. Box 442
Waukon, Iowa 52172-0442
(800) 298-5389
www.kitchenkrafts.com

National Presto Industries
Presto pressure-cookers
and -canners
3925 North Hastings Way
Eau Claire, WI 54703-2209
(800) 877-0441
www.gopresto.com

In Canada

BEEKEEPING

BeeMaid Honey
A complete beekeeping supply
outlet
625 Roseberry Street
Winnipeg, Manitoba
R3G 0T4
(8660) 788-8030 or (204) 786-8977
www.beemaid.com

BEER AND WINE

5gallons.com
A Montreal-based online store
featuring home wine- and beer-
making supplies
(888) 946-3942
www.5gallons.com

GARDENING

Lee Valley Tools Ltd.
Tools, books, and DVDs to help
with fruit and vegetable gardening,
seeding, pruning, and pest control.
Extensive hardware catalog for
custom racks, boxes, and shelving
P.O. Box 6295, Station J
Ottawa, Ont. K2A 1T4
(800) 267-8767 or (613) 596-0350
www.leevalley.com

Salt Spring Seeds
British Columbia-based producers
and suppliers of untreated, non-
GMO seeds for growing many types
of produce
Box 444, Ganges P.O.
Salt Spring Island, B.C.
V8K 2W1
www.saltspringseeds.com

LIVESTOCK

Rochester Hatchery
A family owned hatchery shipping
chicken, pheasant, turkey, and
hybrid hatchlings across Canada
9420 109 Street
Westlock, Alberta
T7P 2R4
www.rochesterhatchery.com

PRESERVING

Golda's Kitchen
An online store featuring a
range of home-canning and
pickling equipment, supplies, and
educational materials
(866) 465-3299
www.goldaskitchen.com

Wellscan Co. Ltd.
An online store offering jars and
food-grade cans, canning devices,
vacuum sealers, jerky kits, smokers,
and dehydrators
8705 Government Street
Burnaby, B.C.
V3N 4G9
(604) 420-0959
www.wellscan.ca

INDEX

Page reference in **boldface**
indicates illustration